The Films of
JOHN GARFIELD

BY
JAMES L. NEIBAUR

Published in the USA by:
BearManor Media
1317 Edgewater Dr #110
Orlando, FL 32804
www.bearmanormedia.com

Perfect ISBN 978-1-62933-842-2
Case ISBN 978-1-62933-843-9

BearManor Media, Orlando, Florida
Printed in the United States of America
Book design by Robbie Adkins, www.adkinsconsult.com

TABLE OF CONTENTS

ACKNOWLEDGEMENTS

First, as always, I have to thank my magnificent assistant Katie Carter, who lives every book with me, watching the films and going over my chapters to fix many typos, offer suggestions, and provide her own insights.

John Garfield's daughter, Julie, has done documentaries and interviews giving special insight to her father's life and career that assisted with this project's accuracy.

Articles and essays by such fine film historians as Kim Morgan, Farran Nehme, and Imogen Sara Smith provided further insight and enlightenment.

Special thanks also to the following for their friendly support, and personal encouragement:
Gary Schneeberger, Terri Lynch, Allie Schulz, Kelly Parmelee, Jill Blake, Ted Okuda, Peter Jackel, Phil Hall, Jim Beaver, Eddie Muller, Dale Wamboldt, Turner Classic Movies, and to the memory of my late son Max Neibaur, who will forever inspire everything I do.

INTRODUCTION

In the comparatively brief time from 1938 to 1951, John Garfield was a movie star, dominating the screen in many films that have become landmark classics. And, despite having died young at only 39, Garfield's impact as an actor has continued to represent some of the finest work in American cinema. His theatrical roots, understanding of method acting, and continued connection to the theater throughout his film career, was the portent for post-war stage-trained actors like Marlon Brando, who redefined screen acting.

John Garfield was the liaison between the earlier tough guy actors like James Cagney, Humphrey Bogart, and Edward G. Robinson; and the brooding actors like Brando and James Dean. He had some of the qualities of the previous, and added the extra traits that would define the later actors. And somehow, he is less noted than the older, or the younger, actors in that connection. Kim Morgan, on her Sunset Gun website, stated it quite well:

> Though he's certainly picked up much more appreciation in the last several years, I still ask: why isn't he supremely famous? Why isn't he a household name? Why isn't he better recognized? For reasons I cannot decipher, this brilliant, brooding actor, though well respected by those who know better, isn't considered the legend a la Bogart, Clift, Brando or Dean. Why isn't he properly appreciated? This massive talent with genuine bad-boy street cred (he was born Julius Garfinkle and raised tough on the streets of Brooklyn and the Bronx) was an acting innnovator and a huge star in his day. So why, aside from true movie lovers, isn't he the huge star he was? He's certainly not dated. Watch Clift, Brando, Dean and other "method" actors and you see Garfield's complex, plain speaking, natural anti-hero influence.[1]

Garfield had been a serious stage actor, belonging to a theatrical group whose members balked when he chose to enter motion pictures. His success on stage caused the studios to court him for some years, but he refused to sign a contract until it was assured that he could take time off to continue pursuing theatrical work. Jack Warner agreed to those

---

1 Morgan, Kim. Happy 100th Birthday John Garfield. Sunset Gun website. March 4, 2013

terms, and Garfield was hired as a featured player at Warner Brothers. After his film debut in *Four Daughters* (1938) was such a sensation he was nominated for an Oscar, the studio immediately elevated him to leading man. The ensuing years with Warner Brothers resulted in the studio casting him in carefully crafted vehicles for an established screen persona, while Garfield wanted to play different roles, exhibit some versatility, and didn't want to be a "type." This resulted in refusals, walkouts, and suspensions until his contract was up in 1946, and Warner Brothers chose not to renew. Garfield entered independent filmmaking with his own production company, resulting in some of his best work as an actor.

This book will be a film-by-film look at the 29 feature films that featured John Garfield throughout his career. Background will be provided for each film, including period reviews, and first-run audience reactions as reported in the trades, as well as a critical assessment. Throughout this study, we will discuss how Garfield responded to formulaic studio films, artistic challenges, and independent production. Early chapters will offer information about his early years and his stage work. The gist of the entire text will be to celebrate the work of a fine actor whose impact still resonates in the 21st century. John Garfield's filmography includes some of cinema's strongest features, including *Pride of the Marines, Gentleman's Agreement, The Postman Always Rings Twice, Body and Soul,* and, his last, *He Ran All the Way,* which culminates Garfield's movie career with one of his finest performances.

While this is not a biography, the book will dispel inaccuracies that have permeated areas of Garfield's life story, while also offering some narrative regarding his personal life. Much of Garfield's work was informed by his politics, while his personal life and, eventually, his career was affected by the political climate of the time. However, because this isn't a biography, this is not the book to get complete information about John Garfield's run-ins with the House UnAmerican Activities Committee. One can consult this book's Bibliography for that information. This book deals specifically with his films, and Garfield's politics will only be discussed as it relates to these films – sometimes this is more extensive than other times.

Film history benefits from a number of exceptional actors and filmmakers who helped develop the language of cinema, or make an impactful presence on the ways and attitudes that crossed over an era. In John Garfield's short career, he went from the pre-war period, the war years, and the post war era; three distinctive periods in American cinema. How is work responded to these eras, to various directors, and to cinema inspired by stage training will all be a part of this study.

THE EARLY YEARS

While this is a film study and not a biography, John Garfield's early life and how its events led him to an interest in theater are part of his screen career's trajectory. John Garfield was born Jacob Julius Garfinkle on Manhattan's Lower East Side on March 4, 1913, and was called Julie by his friends and family. His mother died when he was young; a tumultuous event that would have an effect on his behavior. Young Julie had to jump from relative to relative when not living with his father, and that caused an emotional disruption. Julie was basically a troubled street kid and it was suggested that he be sent to Angelo Patri's school for difficult children. While Julie's dad initially balked at sending his son to what he believed to be a reform school, discussing the institution with Patri changed his mind. Patri ran a good, supportive scholastic program where students' strengths were recognized and cultivated. Patri saw through the unruly young man's belligerence and believed Julie had the sort of personality and charisma that made acting a likely activity. Julie also had a bit of an emotional stammer that was successfully addressed by speech classes. Julie's teacher, Margaret O'Ryan, helped him develop proper speech patterns with exercises and, eventually, assignments where he would address the entire student body. This led to further interest in acting, so Julie started appearing in school plays. After taking second place in a debate competition, the tough, troubled street youth started taking some real pride in his scholastic activities.

This early experience was just the thing the young man needed, as it gave him both confidence and a purpose. In his classes, he could see immediate results and gauge his successes, and this caused the anger in the young man to dissipate. For the remainder of his life, John Garfield would fondly recall how Angelo Parti's school helped him when he was still angry young Julie from the streets.

Garfield eventually moved on to an actual drama school, and soon ended up in the American Laboratory Theater, with Richard Bolesalvsky staging its plays and Maria Ousepenskaya teaching its acting classes. These were the foundational days of Konstantin Stanislavksy's method approach to acting. Along with taking classes, Garfield learned stagecraft, building sets, and encountered such actors as Franchot Tone, Lee Strasberg, and Stella Adler.

In 1931 when his apprenticeship ended, John Garfield looked into securing paying work in some theater companies but to no avail. An offer of a factory job seemed promising, but he wanted it just for the summer, and the employers were looking for someone permanent. Garfield then decided to shuck everything and hitchhike his way to Nebraska where a friend was working in the wheat fields. He would recall years later:

> I think I broke my father's heart leaving like that. But kids are selfish and don't know their cruelty. Out on the road with my thumb waving, suddenly I felt happier than I'd ever been before. What I really wanted was to be on my own, and I saw a turning point.[2]

Garfield spent a year living the vagabond life of a hobo, hopping trains and taking various jobs along the way.

Finding his way back to acting, John Garfield made his Broadway debut in 1932 in the play *Lost Boy* which ran two weeks. With his first credit, Garfield was able to build upon his Broadway experience, however brief, and secured a featured role in a three-month run of "Counselor-at Law" which starred Paul Muni.

Receiving an offer from Warner Brothers, where Muni himself had started making movies, Garfield instead chose to join a new theater set called The Group, which was started by friends Cheryl Crawford and Lee Strasberg. Playwright Clifford Odets, an old friend from the Bronx, had enjoyed success with his one-act play *Waiting for Lefty* and the group decided to produce his next drama *Awake and Sing*. Odets insisted his friend John Garfield play the lead. Opening in 1935, powerful critic Brooks Atkinson took notice of Garfield's performance in his review. Odets was impressed with his friend's work, and wrote the play *Golden Boy* with him in mind. Garfield was quite crestfallen upon hearing that the more established Luther Adler was cast in the lead, and started taking movie acting more seriously as Warner Brothers was still interested.

John Garfield's main problem with appearing in movies was that the studio didn't want to allow him time off to continue to pursue theatrical roles. During these days of the studio system, it was expected that Garfield sign a contract and take whatever roles that Warners felt were right for him. However, the talent Garfield displayed and the notice his stage work was garnering caused the studio to compromise. John Garfield signed a contract as a featured player for seven years with options. At a time when theater people looked down on the movies as inferior,

---

2 Swindell, Larry. *Body and Soul: The Story of John Garfield*. NY: Morrow. 1975

Garfield's colleagues from The Group felt that he'd betrayed his craft. Of course, eventually, many of them would end up in movies as well.

It should be noted that John Garfield did not appear in films before signing with Warner Brothers in 1938. There are several sources that erroneously claim he can be seen in the Busby Berkeley musical *Footlight Parade* (1933). There is a quick one-second cutaway to a closeup of a sailor in James Cagney and Ruby Keeler's "Shanghai Lil" musical number, and he looks like Garfield. But when the film is paused exactly on that shot, it is quite obviously not him.

After the studio renamed Jacob Julius Garfinkle as John Garfield they searched for an appropriate debut vehicle. There were plans to cast him in different projects, and this garnered some publicity, but these reports were just the studio's searching for the right vehicle. That eventually happened with the film *Four Daughters*.

FOUR DAUGHTERS

Directed by Michael Curtiz
Screenplay by Julius J. Epstein and Lenore J. Coffee from a story in *Cosmopolitan* by Fannie Hurst.
Produced by Hal B. Wallis
Cinematography by Ernest Haller
Edited by Ralph Dawson

Cast:
Priscilla Lane, Rosemary Lane, Lola Lane, Gail Page, Claude Rains, Jeffrey Lynn, John Garfield, Frank McHugh, May Robson, Dick Foran, Vera Lewis, Tom Dugan, Eddie Acuff, Donald Kerr, Lillian Lawrence, Wilfred Lucas, Jerry Mandy, Joe Cunningham.

Released August 9, 1938
Warner Brothers
90 minutes
Black and White

John Garfield had a contract with Warner Brothers but they weren't quite sure what to do with him. At first, he was considered for a male role in the Bette Davis vehicle, *The Sisters* (1938), but these plans soon changed. The studio then thought it might be best to expand upon Garfield's being the inspiration for the Clifford Odets play *Golden Boy* and thought a boxing drama might be best. While Garfield did not play the lead in the Broadway production of *Golden Boy*, as Odets intended, he did resonate with a smaller role. Louella Parsons stated in her column:

> I wonder if you remember *The Patent Leather Kid*, a Richard Barthelmess fight movie which he made for Warner Brothers in 1926 with Molly O'Day as his leading lady. It ushered in the first of the pugilistic dramas which later became so popular the box office. Well, to make a long story short, John Garfield, formerly Jules, who played in *Golden Boy* on the stage, will be starred in a remake of Gerald Beaumont's *Patent Leather Kid*. [3]

---

3 Louella Parsons column. *San Francisco Examiner.* June 6, 1938

The studio's plans for John Garfield seemed to be quite plentiful based on an article that appeared in the press about a month after the Parsons column:

> It's enough to make one dizzy, the parts that are, at least alleged-ly, being assigned to John Garfield. There seems to be a real Warner drive on to cast illumination on this young actor. Only a few days ago he was mentioned for young Porfirio Diaz in *Phantom Crown*, and before that is ever started he will be appearing in the lead opposite Rosemary Lane in *Blackwell's Island*, and later on will do *The Sucker*, a prizefight narrative once listed for James Cagney. After which the *Life of Gershwin* and *Patent Leather Kid* are still programmed. That's enough to keep the young player busy for a year.[4]

Some of these projects did indeed come to fruition, some did not. Warner Brothers had no idea how much John Garfield would resonate in his very first movie, which turned out to be *Four Daughters*.

This film version of Fannie Hurst's story *Sister Act* was designed as a vehicle for the Lane Sisters, especially Priscilla, whom the studio was planning to groom for bigger and better things. They gave the project to Michael Curtiz, the studio believing that after his hard work on *Angels With Dirty Faces*, a light, pleasant trifle like this would be a relaxing assignment for him. However, Curtiz took the elements of the story, the screenplay, the characters, and the actors he had to work with and created a film that was one of the studio's biggest hits during a very successful year.

Claude Rains plays Adam Lemp, a music professor who has four daughters that are musical prodigies. The Lemp sisters, Emma (Gale Page), Thea (Lola Lane), Kay (Rosemary Lane), and Ann (Priscilla Lane) spend most of their time exploring their respective musical talents, while also pursuing romance. The Lemps' neighbor Ernest (Dick Foran) is big, handsome, bumbling and earnest, and is in smitten with oldest daughter Emma. Second oldest Thea has been dating an older, plain looking, wealthy man named Ben Crowley (Frank McHugh). Kay is less interested in romance, and more interested in her musical pursuits, which net a scholarship. But Kay is reticent about leaving home. Finally, youngest daughter Ann is a violinist who is initially attracted to Felix Deitz, a tall handsome roomer at the Lemp home, who is also a composer. But when Deitz sends for a wayward friend, orchestral arranger Mickey (John Garfield), she becomes attracted to his rugged, iconoclastic manner as being so much different than the others. Turns out Emma, who rebuffs Ernest's attention, is also in love with Felix. When Ann discovers Emma's affec-

4 Many Roles Lined Up For Garfield. *Los Angeles Times*. July 8, 1938.

tions for Felix, she instead elopes with Mickey. Months go by and Ann and Mickey are broke and unsuccessful, living a life of poverty. Ann shows strength despite Mickey feeling like a failure. At a Christmas gathering with the entire family, it is discovered that Emma and Felix never did get together and she ended up with Ernest after all. Felix is now a success, but lonely. Observing all that is going on, and realizing

Priscilla Lane is attracted to John Garfield in Four Daughters.

he has not been right for Ann, Mickey drives his car recklessly through a snowstorm and crashes it, dying in the hospital not long afterward. Felix and Ann end up together after Mickey's sacrifice.

The way Ann is attracted to Mickey isn't much different than the way movie audiences were attracted to John Garfield when *Four Daughters* hit theaters. After some ballyhoo in the press on how the stage actor was about to debut in movies, and some discussion of different projects line up for him, *Four Daughters* was released. The earlier part of the film introduces all the characters and sets up the narrative. Everyone is clean-cut, well-mannered, and exhibit the sort of exuberant goody-goody qualities that seem to cry out for at least some semblance of conflict or rebellion. Garfield enters and his character of Mickey is a musical genius, who is sarcastic, brooding, and the very antithesis of the setting. However, he is not in conflict with any individual. His sarcasm is met with the same from the Lemp housekeeper Aunt Etta (May Robson), and everyone finds him brilliantly attractive in his own sardonic manner. When he is married and penniless, feeling insecure, he never lashes out angrily at Ann, and she remains supportive. He wisecracks that she must be insane to still love him. His ultimate sacrifice comes off as romantic within the parameters of the narrative.

According to Alan K. Rode's book *Michael Curtiz: A Life in Film*, it was the director who zeroed in on John Garfield's appeal:[5]

> Curtiz and Garfield got on extremely well. Garfield realized that Curtiz knew exactly what he was doing, and the director observed that the young New Yorker who possessed the intangible movie star charisma was dedicated to his craft.

A major part of John Garfield's appeal and part of the brilliance of the way that Garfield plays Mickey, is that behind his hard exterior you can

Despite being broke and despondent, Priscilla Lane and John Garfield remain in love in Four Daughters.

see the softness, especially in his interactions with Ann. This went a long way toward forming the screen persona that we would see from Garfield throughout the remainder of his career.

When Jeffrey Lynn, also a newcomer in films at the time, saw Garfield's screen test when he arrived to do his own, he stated, "that kid's going to steal the picture from all of us." And that is exactly what he does. Garfield

---

5   Rode, Alan K. Michael Curtiz: A Life in Film. University Press of Kentucky, 2017

effortlessly overpowers every scene in which he appears, offsetting the proceedings as a strong, attractive presence. According to Rode:

> Garfield's suicide as Mickey Borden is similarly striking. We see him driving a car with the perspective alternating between his face and his view of the snowy road through the windshield as the wiper sweeps off the snowflakes. Lighting a cigarette with wide-eyed resolve, he switches off the windshield wipers. There is a quick close-up of his foot pushing the accelerator to the floor, then his anguished expression and the windshield turns opaque with snow as the scene dissolves. Billy Wilder remarked that this sequence "was one of the best suicides ever in a picture."[6]

Critics were impressed with *Four Daughters* and most of them pointed out John Garfield's small supporting role for special mention. B.R. Crisler in *The New York Times* stated:

> A charming, at times heartbreakingly human, little comedy about life in a musical family of attractive daughters which occasionally is ruffled by the drama of a masculine world outside, *Four Daughters* tempts one to agree with Jack Warner's recent assertion in the advertisements that it is the climax of his career. Putting aside Mr. Warner's career for the nonce, we may assert with equal confidence that Four Daughters is one of the best pictures of anybody's career, if only for the sake of the marvelously meaningful character of Mickey Borden as portrayed by John Garfield, who bites off his lines with a delivery so eloquent that we still aren't sure whether it is the dialogue or Mr. Garfield who is so bitterly brilliant.[7]

John Garfield was nominated for an Academy Award as Best Supporting Actor. He didn't win, but his immediate impact was enormous.

It should be noted that all of the players are very good in their roles. The Lane sisters, especially Priscilla, resonate as the sisters, as does Gale Page who has the difficult role of balancing both happiness and heartache, both secure and insecure in her choices. Priscilla's exhibition of unconditional love and understanding has a natural quality that never becomes melodramatic, even in sequences where it could have easily lapsed into such a phase. Priscilla Lane has so much chemistry with both Lynn and Garfield that her relationship with, and attraction to, both of them is believable. Dick Foran, who played everything from disgruntled jealous boyfriends to western heroes in Warners B movies, is quite effec-

---

6 Rode, Alan K. *Michael Curtiz: A Life in Film*. University Press of Kentucky, 2017
7 Four Daughters review. *The New York Times*. August 19, 1938

tive as the bumbling Ernest, while Frank McHugh is far more subdued than the comic support he plays in other films. Jeffrey Lynn is handsome and appealing, but in a stiffer and less charismatic way, causing Garfield to shine even more brightly. And old pros like Claude Rains and May Robson have no trouble keeping up with the younger cast.

His performance in *Four Daughters* caused Warner Brothers to realize that John Garfield was more than a featured player. They revised his contract, elevating him from featured player to star player for seven years with no options. Upon completing *Four Daughters*, but before its release, Garfield had completed a B movie, *Blackwell's Island*, where he didn't even have the lead role, By the time it was ready for release, Garfield's impact in *Four Daughters* had made its impact. Warner Brothers did not want a star player to be in a lower budgeted film, so they withdrew *Blackwell's Island* in order to expand both its budget and Garfield's role by shooting some new scenes, elevating it to A-picture status. In the meantime, Warner Brothers cast John Garfield in his own starring vehicle, a boxing drama entitled *They Made Me a Criminal.*

THEY MADE ME A CRIMINAL

Directed by Busby Berkeley
Screenplay by Sid Herzig from a novel and play by Bertram Millhauser
and Beulah Marie Dix.
Produced by Hal B. Wallis
Cinematography by James Wong Howe
Edited by Jack Kilifer

Cast:
John Garfield, Gloria Dickson, Claude Rains, The Dead End Kids (Billy
Halop, Leo Gorcey, Bobby Jordan, Huntz Hall, Gabe Dell, Bernard Pun-
sley), May Robson, Ann Sheridan, Louis Jean Heydt, Robert Glecker,
John Ridgely, Barbara Pepper, William Davidson, Ward Bond, Robert
Strange, Frank Riggi, Cliff Clark, Dick Wessel, Leyland Hodgson, Sam
Hayes, Nat Carr, Arthur Housman, Sam McDaniel, Bert Roach, Ronald
Sinclair, Tom Wilson, John Dilson, Mushy Callahan, Irving Bacon, Rich-
ard Bond, Hal Craig, Eddy Chandler, Tom Dugan, Paul Panzer, John
Harron, Jimmy O'Gatty, Jack Mower, Stuart Holmes, Frank Meredith,
Donald Kerr, Larry McGrath, Reid Kilpatrick, Harry LeRoy, Frank
Mayo, Art Lloyd, Bob Perry, Jack Wise, Charles Randolph, Dorothy Var-
den, Elliot Sullivan, Cyril Ring, Sally Sage, John J. Richardson, Charles
Sullivan, Janet Shaw, Dave Roberts, Jack Austin, Georgie Cooper.

Released January 28, 1939
Warner Brothers
92 minutes
Black and White

With John Garfield's completed B movie *Blackwell's Island* pulled from
distribution so that it could be expanded to A-level status, Warner Brothers hurried the actor into his first starring vehicle. Garfield was cast in
what originally was to be called *The Sucker* and star James Cagney. *They
Made Me a Criminal* had been filmed before in 1933 as *The Life of Jimmy
Dolan* with Douglas Fairbanks jr. in the lead role.

Warner Brothers further tried to ensure the film's success by adding
both Claude Rains and May Robson from *Four Daughters* to the cast of
They Made Me a Criminal. Robson was comfortably cast as a no-non-

John Garfield had his first starring role in They Made Me a Criminal.

sense grandmother type, but Rains thought he was all wrong for the role of a wise-cracking detective. He initially refused the role, but the studio threatened to suspend him, so he accepted it. For the rest of his life, Rains would refer to this part as his worst, but John Garfield felt that Rains was excellent in the role and stole the picture.

William Beaudine was first announced as the film's director. Beaudine had scored with several popular films throughout the silent era and early 1930s, until 1935 when he went to direct several films in England. Returning to America, Beaudine had lost his status in the business, and the only work he could get was directing a couple of B-level movies in Warners' Torchy Blaine series. When these proved successful, Beaudine was considered a good director for *They Made Me a Criminal*, because he was noted for being able to successfully direct younger actors, and The Dead End Kids had been cast in the film. The Dead Enders had been good box office, but difficult to control on the set. Beaudine's reputation indicated that he would indeed be able to control them, and direct an efficient production. However, while William Beaudine did not direct the *They Made Me a Criminal*, a few years later he began directing a few of the Dead End Kids in their low budget series The East Side Kids, and would be a major factor in developing their popular Bowery Boys series of the post-war era and 1950s.

The reason Beaudine did not end up helming *They Made Me a Criminal* is because the studio needed something for musical director Busby Berkeley, who was coming to the end of his Warner Brothers contract. The lavish backstage musicals Berkeley specialized in, including the classics *42nd Street* (1932) and *Footlight Parade* (1933), had faded in popularity by the end of the 1930s. The director was longing to helm a non-musical feature, so the studio gave him this assignment. As it turned out, he was not the only director who ended up working on this project.

Producers considered casting Priscilla Lane in the leading lady role, because she and John Garfield had worked so well together in *Four Daughters*. However, the studio wanted to groom Lane for bigger things, and the role in *They Made Me a Criminal* was a part for a featured player. As a result, Gloria Dickson, who had just appeared with Humphrey Bogart in a popular B movie, *Racket Busters* (1938), was cast.

John Garfield plays left-handed prizefighter Johnnie Bradfield who is marketed as a wholesome type who frequently mentions his beloved mother's positive influence. After a fight, while carrying on drunkenly with his girl (Ann Sheridan) and a couple of her friends, Bradfield reveals he has no mother and that it's all a ruse. It is discovered that one member of the party is a reporter. Johnnie tries to get him to keep quiet about the story, but the reporter sees a scoop. There is a scuffle and Johnnie drunkenly conks out, while his manager hits the reporter with a bottle and kills him. An incoherent Johnnie is brought to a hideout, and his manager runs away with his girl. They are killed in an accident, and when Johnnie awakens a few days later, he discovers via newspapers that it is believed to have been killed in the crash, and also that he was responsible for the reporter's murder. The manager had stolen Johnnie's car, and his watch, so this is now the badly burned body was identified. Johnnie changes his name to Jack Dorney and escapes into the life of a vagabond, staying on the backroads to avoid being recognized. He ends up on a farm in Arizona, where an older woman (May Robson) has taken in several delinquents (The Dead End Kids) to work on the farm. Peggy (Gloria Dickson), a sister of one of the boys, is their guardian and also lives on the farm. When money is needed, Johnnie sees a barnstorming fighter is taking on all comers at a carnival nearby and plans to enter, realizing he can win such a match with little effort. Meanwhile, a detective (Claude Rains), is not convinced Johnnie was killed in the car, because the dead man had the watch on the wrong hand, and the fighter was a noted southpaw. His investigation leads him to the fight Johnnie is in, recognizing his odd southpaw stance in a newspaper article. The detective is at the show, so Johnnie spends the entire bout fighting right-handed, which gives his far less skilled opponent the edge. When he is about to lose the fight, the detective informs him that he knows who he is the ruse is unnecessary. Johnnie switches his stance and wins the fight. But he is expected to go with the detective and go on trial for the reporter's murder. Haunted by a bad decision in his past that sent an innocent man to the electric chair,

Gloria Dickson and John Garfield with The Dead End Kids: Bernard Punsley, Billy Halop, Huntz Hall, Bobby Jordan, Leo Gorcey, Gabe Dell.

the detective lets Johnnie go at the last minute.

It is surprising that *They Made Me a Criminal* comes off so successfully as its production was so troubled, it took three directors to put it together. An article in the press stated:

> *They Made Me a Criminal* is being almost completely remade. At the beginning, back in August, May Robson was playing an important role but had to leave the cast when she broke an arm. So, Beulah Bondi was rushed into the part and Miss Robson 's scenes were shot again. The picture was completed that way, and then the studio decided that Miss Bondi didn't look old enough.

Miss Robson had recovered by that time, so she returned and the role was filmed a third time at an added cost of $150,000. If the picture doesn't click it won't be because they haven't used plenty of people. Busby Berkeley was the director at first, but he's off the studio payroll. Michael Curtiz made several weeks of retakes with Miss Bondi, and now William Keighley is directing what should be the final version.[8]

Despite these disruptions, *They Made Me a Criminal* is a strong drama with several scenes that can be considered highlights.

John Garfield's acting is given more of an opportunity to shine, in that he appears in nearly every scene. He has to convey the gamut of emotions and he does so quite effectively. The character of Johnnie is an actor himself. The boxer's ring persona is one of a clean-living, mother-loving good guy – an example of a wholesome All American who is above reproach. Johnnie must convey this effectively, and he does well enough to fool reporters as well as fans. The idea that he is, in fact, a motherless, hard-drinking womanizer would be a huge story, since he has some celebrity in the boxing world. So naturally the reporter has to embrace it as a scoop.

Garfield's presenting Johnnie's shift from his good boy persona to the drunken womanizer is less abrupt than generally cynical in the gritty Warner Brothers tradition, but his acting is especially impressive when he awakens and starts to piece together what has gone on. Garfield exhibits the confusion, and the fear, that the scene calls for, with a natural flair that extends beyond the character-driven stylistic approach of, say, an Edward G. Robinson. It is the method-trained bridge to how movie acting would be redefined in the post-war era. This emotional response is revisited when vagabond Johnnie runs into trouble at a diner, and is ready to fight, but must back down so as not to be recognized for his noticed stance and style.

The Dead End Kids had been in movies for a few years, debuting in Samuel Goldwyn's *Dead End* (1937) after having appeared in the play. At Warner Brothers they continued their success with films like *Crime School* (1938) and *Angels With Dirty Faces* (1938), often being very difficult to contain by directors, while actors found that their ad-libbing often made knowing dialog cues difficult. When they tried this in *Angels With Dirty Faces*, the film's star James Cagney, a no-nonsense actor who was a genuine street kid himself, punched Leo Gorcey after an ad-lib and, according to Bernard Punsley, "Word came down from Gorcey not to mess with

---

8 Paul Harrison in Hollywood. NEA syndicate. January 9, 1939

14

Cagney."[9]   In the case of John Garfield, another tough street kid, the dynamic was much different.   Cagney was old enough to be the Kids' father.   Garfield was only a few years older than the oldest Dead Ender, so they connected as peers and got along quite well.   Garfield would even

John Garfield and Gloria Dickson bid farewell as Claude Rains waits nearby in They Made Me a Criminal.

point out in press interviews how great they were as actors.

It can perhaps be somewhat understanding why Claude Rains felt mis-cast as a fast-talking detective, mostly because his diction is that of an orator and not a cynical cop. However, the character he plays is troubled, haunted by a bad decision, introspective and brooding. Rains was brilliant with subtle nuance and even gave John Garfield advice as to how to respond to the intimate camera during close-ups; something stage actors, used to broad gestures for the back row, never fully master. It is Rains' gift for nuance that makes his performance far better than he ever believed it to be.

Shooting *They Made Me a Criminal* was quite grueling for the cast, as the heat on the farm location could reach 120 degrees Fahrenheit and the area was besieged by annoying gnats. When a correspondent for the

---

9   Walker, Brent and David Haynes. *The Films of the Bowery Boys.* Secaucus, NJ: Citadel, 1981

movie trade magazine *Silver Screen* visited the set, they took note of the difficult conditions and indicated that Garfield seemed unflinching about the location and genuinely surprised at his immediate success:

> He is still unspoiled by success. Most of the boys and girls who shoot up fast really are spoiled, but not John Garfield. He thinks it's more or less of a miracle that's happened to him. He's living very modestly in a rented Hollywood house. He's dark haired, brown eyed, and is somewhat shorter than the average film star, standing only 5 feet 9 inches. But he's dynamic and when you see him on screen you forget that anybody else is up there playing the scene with him.[10]

Garfield, still new to the moviemaking process, was eager to tell the correspondent about his first time working on location:

> We started away from Hollywood in a lengthy motorcade. There was at the head of the line, a sound truck carrying the dialog recording apparatus, and then a generator truck to develop the necessary electricity. And a camera truck, and then several more big five-tonners that tranpsorted the lights and properties. There were three huge busses, each carrying twenty-five or thirty extra players, and seven company cars for the principals and the rest of the cast. And there was a wardrobe truck as well as three station wagons, one of them used to carry back each night the film we shot during the day, so it may be developed and printed and viewed by executives in the studio projection room.[11]

Garfield also stated that it got so hot during shooting that sometimes the film actually melted inside the camera.

They Made Me a Criminal was a hit, and it confirmed the studio's belief that John Garfield was their new young star. They next planned to co-star John Garfield with James Cagney in the prison drama *Each Dawn I Die*, with Garfield playing a crusading reporter who is framed, and Cagney the benevolent gangster who helps him clear his name. However, Cagney was promised a six-week vacation after completing his latest movie, *The Oklahoma Kid*, and so Garfield signed on to return to Broadway in *Heavenly Express*. The movie was changed to where Cagney was now in the role of the reporter, and both Humphrey Bogart and Edward G. Robinson were announced in the press as being considered for the role of the gangster, until the studio settled on George Raft.

---

10 122 Degrees. *Silver Screen.* January, 1939
11 122 Degrees. *Silver Screen.* January, 1939

While Garfield was appearing on Broadway, Warners released the retooled *Blackwell's Island* and searched for the appropriate property to feature their new star.

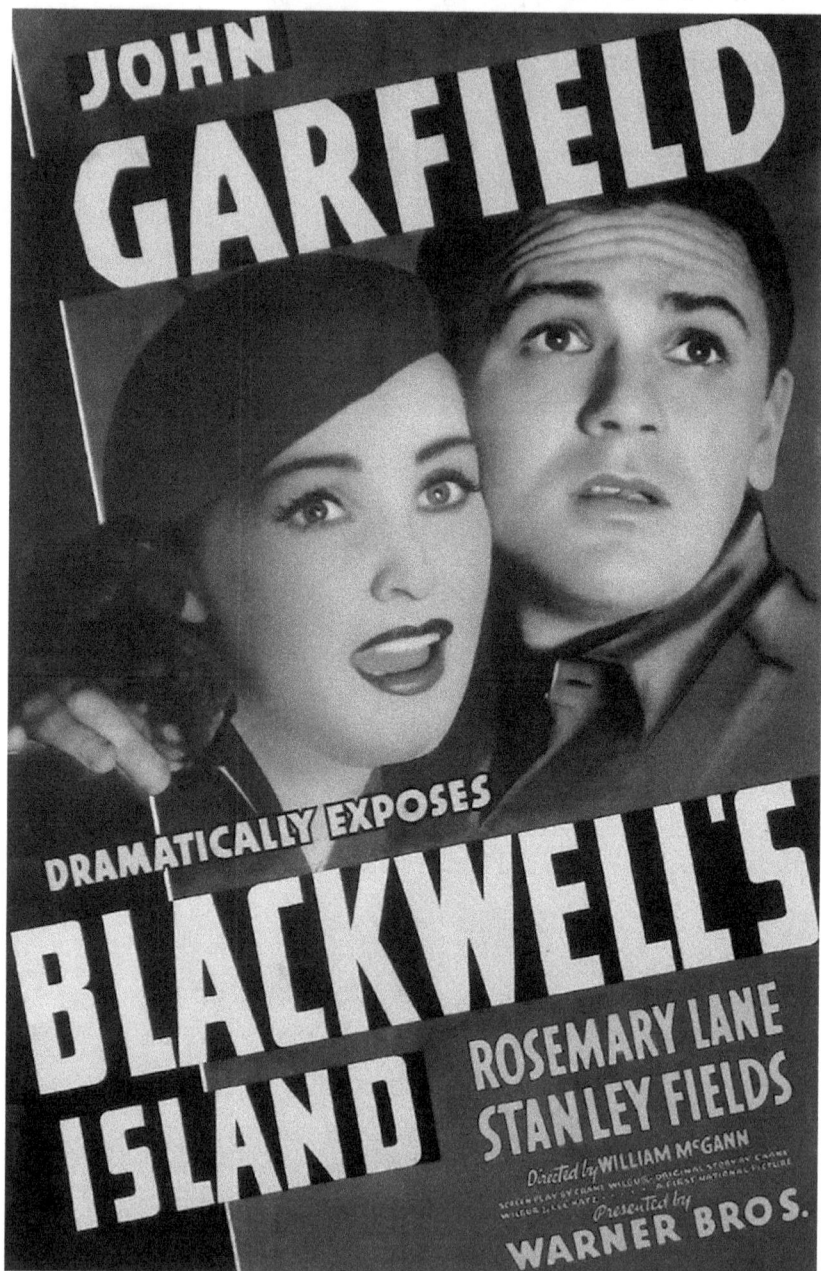

Although he received star–billing, John Garfield is only a supporting player in
Blackwell's Island.

BLACKWELL'S ISLAND

Directed by William McGann
Director of additional scenes: Michael Curtiz
Screenplay by Crane Wilbur
Produced by Bryan Foy
Cinematography by Sidney Hickox
Edited by Doug Gould

Cast:
John Garfield, Rosemary Lane, Dick Purcell, Victor Jory, Stanley Fields, Morgan Conway, Granville Bates, Anthony Averill, Peggy Shannon, Charley Foy, Norman Willis, Joe Cunningham, Wade Boteler, William B. Davidson, John Dilson, Chester Gan, Sam Jackson, Brenda Marshall, Jimmy O'Gatty, Herbert Rawlinson, Milburn Stone, Lottie Williams, Walter Young, Leon Ames, Raymond Bailey, Jack Gardner, Sam Bernard, Eddie Foster, James Blaine, Demtris Emanuel, Frank Bruno, Joe De Stefani, Monte Vandergrift, Robert Homans, James Spottswood, Fred Malatesta, Charles Seel, Herman Marks, Dick Rich, Walter Miller, George Guhl, Eddy Chandler, Lew Harvey, Harry Cody, Vera Lewis, Harry Harvey.

Released March 25, 1939
Warner Brothers
71 minutes
Black and White

Blackwell's Island was originally announced in the trades as a late 1938 release, but it was withheld for re-tooling once John Garfield's performance in *Four Daughters* elevated him from featured player to star. *Blackwell's Island* started off as a B movie and after hiring Michael Curtiz to expand its production and shoot a few new scenes, it is still a B movie, even if it could now secure A-movie bookings. *Blackwell's Island* is aggressively entertaining, gives the lead role to character actor Stanley Fields, and breezes by in just over an hour. *Blackwell's Island* is an entertaining movie, but, even with the new scenes, it is of little overall consequence to John Garfield's budding screen career.

John Garfield plays a crusading reporter trying to expose corruption in Blackwell's Island.

Stanley Fields plays Bull Bransom, a racketeer who has risen up in the political world to where he has connections at every level. When he and his mob end up in prison, they take over the infirmary and make it a veritable hotel suite, where they have card games, play the radio, and indulge in other delicacies. Bransom even brings his two Great Dane pet dogs with him, and feeds them steak while the prisoners in general population get slop. John Garfield plays an investigative reporter who gets himself sent to the same prison to he can investigate conditions and eventually report them to the corrections commissioner.

Even though his part has been expanded, John Garfield still appears to be a supporting player while Stanley Fields is the lead role that is central to the movie's narrative. Fields plays Bull as an overgrown child, delighting in practical jokes, struggling with the most basic literacy, and enjoying electric trains and other childlike amusements. Fields' deep voice lends itself well to a "dees-dems-dose" way of speaking, and he defines his character with experience and skill. Fields had played similar characters for drama (*Little Caesar* (1930) with Edward G, Robinson), and comedy (*Way Out West* (1937) with Laurel and Hardy), so he is quite comfortable in the role.

John Garfield's youthful exuberance is certainly entertaining and appealing, but clearly in support of Stanley Fields. This has all the markings of a B movie, right down to being produced by Bryan Foy, the studio's head of B-level film production. Foy, one of the original Seven Little

Foys of vaudeville, had produced some of Warners' early sound Vitaphone shorts, as well as the first all talking feature *Lights of New York*. He was hired to head their B picture unit in 1936, usually in an effort to produce the sort of cheap, aggressive entertainment that was economical to create and paid off nicely on double bills or in neighborhood movie houses. The same year he produced *Blackwell's Island*, Foy was also behind the production of entires in the Nancy Drew, Torchy Blaine, and Dead End Kids series.

Having all of the earmarks of a shorter-length feature to support the main one in a double-feature, *Blackwell's Island* was a bit of a disappointment when securing the top spot on theater programs. Exhibiters complained in the trades that it was too short, and that the actors who received star billing were subordinate to one billed in support (leading lady Rosemary Lane, as a nurse, barely registers at all).

The cast is filled with B-picture stalwarts, including Dick Purcell as a brave cop who stands up to the rackets, Victor Jory as the commissioner, and Granville Bates as the fluttery warden who is more interested in tending to the plants in his office rather than the inmates in his prison.

According to Alan K. Rode's book *Michael Curtiz: A Life in Film*, the climactic boat chase that caps the film was the director's major contribution:

> The picture foundered under the uncertain direction of William C. McGann, who was removed after filming three different endings – all deemed unsatisfactory. Warner did not want his newest star appearing in a bad programmer, but was unwilling to lose money by canceling a nearly completed film. He ordered Curtiz to fix the picture. Curtiz directed a week of retakes in September of 1938. His work included the staging of a climactic speedboat sequence. The result was a lively 71 minute diversion that did no harm to either Garfield's career or the studio's reputation. What was initially viewed as a potential embarrassment grossed a quarter million dollars over its modest cost.[12]

While there is a significant amount of action and drama (including a couple of murders), *Blackwell's Island* plays as a comedy. Fields performs as a comic character whose manner and actions are more laughable than they are sinister, despite his organizing such crimes as planting a bomb on a dead man's body in an attempt to kill the cop, the reporter, and the nurse all at the same time. Frank S. Nugent in *The New York Times* stated:

> There is bitter laughter in the phenomenon of a protected mobster accepting a face-saving six-month rap in jail and dictat-

---

12 Rode, Alan K. Michael Curtiz: A Life in Film. University Press of Kentucky, 2017

ing his terms to a pension-conscious warden. We can grin, rue-fully, at the sight of convicts making book on the races, playing poker, lolling about in striped silk pajamas, ordering the keepers about like lackeys. The Warners find it laughable and so, reluctantly, must we.[13]

While *Film Daily* admitted:

The manner in which the gangster takes over the prison, and orders the warden and all the guards around, runs a protective association for the prisoners, and installs a private club with all conveniences for himself and his pals, is pretty far-fetched. They even have a direct wire to the racetrack, apparently, for they are making book every day.[14]

Despite lackluster reviews and disappointed exhibitors, *Blackwell's Island* was a hit in spite of itself, and John Garfield remained popular with moviegoers.

It is amusing that critics found the premise of *Blackwell's Island* far-fetched in that it was based on a true story of gangsters taking over a prison, which forced its closure in 1934. Warners even put up a disclaimer at the beginning of the movie to avoid possible lawsuits. The greater irony is that the New York Board of Censors had the film temporarily removed from being shown at the city's Globe theater because they felt it was detrimental to show law enforcement accepting bribes from racketeers. It was returned to the Globe shortly after this absurd claim, and broke box office records at that theater.

While Warner Brothers was preparing John Garfield's next movie project, Columbia Pictures asked to borrow him for their screen version of Clifford Odets' *Golden Boy*, as per the playwright's recommendation. Warners, however, balked at allowing their new star to have a likely box office hit with another studio, so they refused to loan him out. This upset Garfield, who saw it as an opportunity to finally play the lead that had eluded him on stage. The role went to newcomer William Holden.

Plans were then to have Garfield appear in support of Paul Muni and Bette Davis in *Juarez*. Muni had worked with Garfield on stage, and requested that the actor be cast. Garfield coveted the role, but the studio was again concerned for a couple of reasons. First, the very fact that it was a supporting role was beneath what a star player should be doing. Also, it was too much of a departure from the kind of part Garfield had been playing, and they were trying to cultivate an image.

---

13 Blackwell's Island review. *The New York Times*. March 2, 1939
14 Blackwell's Island review. *Film Daily*. March 2, 1939

John Garfield wasn't interested in cultivating an image. As a method-trained stage actor, he was more concerned about branching out, and playing different types of roles and across varying genres. With the help of Muni's clout, and Garfield's own insistence on being allowed to stretch a bit as a screen actor, the studio reneged, and *Juarez* became John Garfield's next movie.

JUAREZ

Directed by William Dieterle
Screenplay by John Huston, Aeneas Mackenzie, Wolfgang Reinhardt, based on the play by Franz Werfel and the novel by Bertita Harding.
Produced by Hal B. Wallis
Cinematography by Tony Gaudio
Edited by Warren Low

Cast:
Paul Muni, Bette Davis, Brian Aherne, Claude Rains, John Garfield, Donald Crisp, Joseph Calleia, Gale Sondergaard, Gilbert Roland, Henry O'Neill, Harry Davenport, Louis Calhern, Walter Kingsford, Georgia Caine, Montagu Love, John Miljan, Vladmir Sokoloff, Irving Pichel, Pedro de Cordoba, Gilbert Emery, Monte Blue, Manuel Diaz, Hugh Sothern, Mickey Kuhn, William Wilkerson, Martin Garralaga, Frank Lackteen, Claudia Dell, Noble Johnson, Frank Reicher, Walter Fenner, Alexander Leftwich, Pedro Regas, Fred Malatesta, Lillian Nicholson, Walter Stahl, Douglas Wood, Paul Porcasi, Robert Warwick, William Edmunds, Guy Bates Post, Stuart Holmes.

Released June 10, 1939
Warner Brothers
125 minutes
Black and White

Paul Muni was one of Warner Brothers' most prestigious stars when he was cast in the title role of this lavish period piece. Bette Davis was given the female lead, and although it was a supporting part where she would be second-billed, she accepted the coveted role. The movie, overall, is very good, benefiting from William Dieterle's skilled direction and the fine performances of both Paul Muni and Bette Davis. However, John Garfield is miscast, and is truly the weak link in this otherwise expansive and beautiful production.

Paul Muni plays Benito Juarez, the President of Mexico, and Brian Aherne is Maximilian I, who is the ruler installed by Napoleon III (Claude Rains). The story is about how Napoleon III, who fears losing the country for France, circumvents the Monroe Doctrine and controlling an election that places his puppet leader Maximilian in charge. Maximil-

John Garfield wanted to act in Juarez, *despite it being a smaller role, but was decidedly miscast.*

ian, arriving in the country with wife Carlota (Bette Davis) discovers that he is expected to seize land that Juarez had given to the citizens, and initiate a French supremacy. Maximillian refuses, and plans to abdicate, but is advised by Carlota to stay and fight for the Mexican citizens. Juarez turns down Maximillian's offer of prime minister, and the Americans plan to support Juarez's efforts by sending arms. The American ammunition is stolen by Vice President Uradi (Joseph Calleia) to help Maximillian achieve victory. Napoleon then removes all French troops from Mexico and Maximillian is without an army. Maximillian and his men are captured and face execution.

According to Margarita Landazuri at the TCM website: "*Juarez* was actually shot as two films, with the Maximilian-Carlotta story shot first. Then it was shown to Muni, and he made notes on further script changes before he shot the Juarez sequences. Then the two stories were intercut in the editing process. Some believe this anomaly in the screenplay ultimately doomed the film to failure, since its two protagonists never confront each other." However, despite this unusual structure, *Juarez* holds up well and was a hit at the box office.

John Garfield is cast as freedom fighter Porfirio Diaz, and has a small role. And despite his method acting skills, Garfield has a lot of trouble overcoming his strong Bronx accent when trying to play the head of the Mexican army. Most reviews barely mentioned him at all.

Pat Patterson, property man for Warner Brothers, told *Photoplay* that obtaining necessary props for the film could sometimes be daunting:

> No matter what's called for, we've got to get it. When Dieterle wanted John Garfield to eat Mexican corn in his cell, we had to scout around for it. Corn was out of season, but there's no such word as 'can't' in the movie industry. We finally located the corn in the agricultural experimental station at the University of California at four dollars an ear, plus postage. Garfield consumed at least a dozen ears for one scene alone, and it took three days to shoot.[15]

John Garfield might not have been the most significant performer in *Juarez*, but it did inspire some interest in Mexico and its people. According to *Silver Screen*:

> All the while he was working in *Juarez*, John Garfield never got any closer than the San Fernando Valley. But the picture made him extremely Mexico-conscious, so when the studio permitted him a three-week vacation recently, he and his wife set out for Mexico City. When he dropped by the table in the Green Room at the studio to tell Olivia de Havilland, one of his favorite actresses goodbye, Olivia turned to her guests and said, "John is going to Mexico to get atmosphere for his last picture."[16]

---

15 Juarez – The Life History of a Movie. *Photoplay.* June, 1939
16 Topics For Gossip. *Silver Screen.* September, 1939

Although *Juarez* is a fairly good movie of its kind, in a book discussing the films of John Garfield, it is of little note. It is a small role that does not feature the actor as anywhere near his best.

John Garfield's next project is a most curious one. The popularity of *Four Daughters* resulted in plans to make a sequel, *Four Wives* with the same cast. However, the studio was unsettled about the fact that John Garfield, the actor most responsible for the first film's success, could not appear in the sequel, because his character had been killed off in the previous one. Jack Warner even made such ridiculous suggestions as Garfield's character having a twin brother, or making him a spirit who watches over the others.

One of Warner's crazy ideas was to gather the cast of *Four Daughters* and make a new movie about different people, albeit with a similar dynamic. The same screenwriters were employed to create a movie from a play by Dorothy Bennett. Michael Curtiz was hired to direct. Claude Rains was cast as the wayward father of four girls, again played by the Lane sisters and Gale Page. Jeffrey Lynn, Frank McHugh, and Dick Foran were all added to the cast. And so was John Garfield. They even titled the film *Daughters Courageous*.

DAUGHTERS COURAGEOUS

Directed by Michael Curtiz
Screenplay by Jules Epstein and Phillip Epstein based on the play *Fly Away Home* by Dorothy Bennett and Irving White
Produced by Hal B. Wallis
Cinematography by James Wong Howe
Edited by Ralph Dawson

Cast:
John Garfield, Claude Rains, Priscilla Lane, Lola Lane, Rosemary Lane, Gale Page, Fay Bainter, Donald Crisp, May Robson, Frank McHugh, Dick Foran, Jeffrey Lynn, George Humbert, Berton Churchill, Jack Gardner, Tom Dugan, Ray Cooke, George Chesbro, Maris Wrixton, George O'Hanlon, Tom Wilson, Leland Hodgson, Leo White, Stuart Holmes, Tom Quinn, William Hopper, Harold Miller, Paul Panzer, Nat Carr, James Millican, Hobart Cavanaugh, Harold Miller, Alice Conners, Bill Edwards, Stuart Holmes.

Released July 22, 1939
Warner Brothers
107 minutes
Black and White

After having proven himself to be a leading man in *Four Daughters,* it is curious as to why John Garfield has a rather small, but pivotal, role in *Daughters Courageous,* especially since he receives top billing. Perhaps the studio felt that Garfield had been the reason for the success of *Four Daughters* and was the star attraction, despite a very competent cast.

Claude Rains plays Jim Masters, an irresponsible wanderer who returns home after a 20-year absence, after having been legally declared dead. He discovers that his daughters are now grown and his wife is prepared to remarry. The youngest daughter, Buff Masters (Priscilla Lane), parallels her mother's youthful choice in Jim by falling for wayward schemer Gabriel Lopez (John Garfield). Each of the diverse characters has their own story to fit into the narrative, which resolves conclusively due to the fine performances, expert direction, and strong screenplay.

Daughters Courageous opens with some amusing, lighthearted scenes that establish the characters and the settings, indicating the mother, Nan

Daughters Courageous *newspaper ad, playing up the familiar cast.*

John Garfield and Priscilla Lane are reunited in Daughters Courageous.

Masters (Fay Bainter) plans to marry her long time beau Sam Sloane (Donald Crisp), who is a sober, conservative businessman. When Jim Masters returns home, he initially doesn't know which daughter is which. When company comes over, they all sit together around the fireplace and kibbitz, while Masters sits alone on another side of the room.

Although he is second-billed, Claude Rains is the real star of *Daughter's Courageous*. He sets the template for the scenes once he enters the film as the wandering father returning after twenty years away. The backstory explains that he simply left, unable to contain his wanderlust, despite having a wife and four small daughters. The character should be considered despicable, but a combination of the writing, direction, and

Rains' performance forces us to admire Jim Masters just as effectively as his charm wins over the daughters, who initially put up a unified front to give him the cold shoulder.

The scene in which the family gathers around the fireplace is beautifully shot by director Michael Curtiz. The family is in the foreground, their conversation and camaraderie showing subtle movement, while Rains sits, very still, in the background, observing. Partly due to the actor's charisma, and partly the framing by the director, but our attention is drawn to Rains and past the rest of the cast. When Rains calls attention to himself by turning on a nearby radio, director Curtiz moves to a closeup.

Despite his role being a smaller supporting one, John Garfield's performance is discernibly impactful as the wayward Gabriel, a cavalier sort who doesn't care much about anything that comes near personal responsibility. He doesn't work, he doesn't respond well to polite society, he makes his money from schemes, and he appears as having a constant chip on his shoulder. He is attracted to Buff, but is rivaled by a staid playwright (Jeffrey Lynn) who, despite his arts-oriented position, is far more solid and successful than Gabriel. The playwright doesn't show much interest in Buff at the start of the film. There's a wonderful scene toward the beginning of the movie when he takes Buff aside and tells her that he loves her. She appears to be won over, as is the audience—but then he reveals that he was just trying out a scene for his play. It's a great gag, as he also appears completely oblivious to what he was doing and how Buff could potentially really care for him

One of the things that appears to especially attract Buff is how Gabriel obviously likes her, but doesn't appear to care if it is reciprocated. For instance, when Gabriel ends up at a dance hall where she is with the playwright, and is informed that he will also be taking her home, he appears to be fine with that and leaves. It is his appearing to not care that attracts Buff away from a man who is very clear that he does.

This connects to Buff's mother and father's relationship. Mother Nan clearly wants Buff to avoid Gabriel completely because his waywardness reminds her of Jim. Jim, however, connects with Gabriel and is comfortable with the relationship. Sam naturally sides with Nan.

Daughters Courageous spends more time with Jim Masters charming his way into the hearts of the daughters than it does with Buff and Gabriel's romance. Sam Slone is powerless against the biological bond, as well as the effortless charisma Jim exudes. He can benefit them with money and opportunity – giving one daughter the money to attend an expensive University, and setting up another's fiancée with a Vice President job in his company. But he hasn't the smooth eloquence that Masters easily commands. There is a powerful emotional scene where Sloane and Masters talk together, with Sam admitting that he can't compete with Jim's presence and, since he is marrying Nan and will be the father figure in the household, he asks that Masters please allow him his place.

Another strong scene in the film occurs when Masters, now having comfortably settled back into family life after two weeks, asks Nan to let him stay. Nan, who is the one individual that never warmed back up to her ex-husband, explains that if he wants to do what is best for his daughters, he should leave. He agrees to do so. Along with the performances and Michael Curitz's succession of shots, this scene benefits from well-written dialog that never gets sloppy. Jim reveals that his 20 years of travels were mostly spent in drab hotels and cheerless train cars.

However, perhaps the most powerful scene of all is when Jim and Gabriel meet and talk. John Garfield spits out his dialog as Gabriel angrily responds to his own place in society:

> You kicked around the world all this time and got nothing out of it at all. You ever see so much hate in this world? Who sets it off and why? I'm stuck here and don't know from nothing. But I'm going to get out. They don't keep Gabriel Lopez down. I wanna get enough dough to get out of here. Not be stuck here like my pop who worked all his life, and has nothing to show for it except sweat and a son like me.

Jim Masters understands Gabriel's feelings, even though they are less pragmatic – they are still just as emotionally impulsive: "You know we're not so far apart. We both suffer from wanderlust. Although, I must say, you've got it with trimmings."

While in *Four Daughters* the Garfield character made the ultimate sacrifice with his life for the girl and the other guy (played by the same two actors), in *Daughters Courageous* it is Claude Rains' character whose last act is a noble one. He leaves behind a note indicating that "two weeks was long enough to stay anywhere" so the daughters would not realize he wanted to stay and their mother convinced him to leave. Meanwhile, Buff has arranged to meet up with Gabriel and elope (as the same two actors' characters did in *Four Daughters*) but another strong scene shows Jim Masters meeting with Gabriel and talking him out of it. Responding to Masters saying, "I don't want you to marry my daughter," Gabriel indicates how he has been working a job responsibly, wearing neckties, and watching his language, all because of Buff. Masters realizes that won't last. He explains this from his own experience. Thus, when Buff is shown waiting for him at the agreed meeting place, the playwright shows up, and tells her that Gabriel came to see him and sent him there. Jeffrey Lynn once again plays the man who gets the girl.

To tie up all loose ends, as Masters prepares to board the train and leave town, he is met by Gabriel who decides to go with him. As the family back home prepares for the wedding between Nan and Sam, they stop as they hear the train whistle in the background as it leaves town.

Moviegoers were not at all confused by *Daughters Courageous* not being a sequel to *Four Daughters* despite the similar title and same cast. Newspaper articles explained the dynamic so that the movie would be accepted on its own. One press released indicated:

> Among the players and technicians concerned in the filming of Daughters Courageous were two winners for the 1938 Academy Awards and four other persons who were nominated for Oscars. The prize winners were Fay Bainter, gold statuette winner for her performance in Jezebel, and Ralph Dawson, winner of the award for film cutting, based on his editing of the spectacular The Adventures of Robin Hood. In Daughters Courageous, Miss Bainter plays the sprightly mother of Rosemary, Priscilla, Lola Lane and Gale Page, while Dawson was in charge of cutting the picture to its final form. Michael Curtiz, the director, directed two of the five pictures which were nominated for consideration as 1938's best directorial achievements. The other nominees were John Garfield, featured player in Four Daughters last year; scenarist Jules Epstein, who did the script for Four Daughters, and cameraman Ernest Haller, who did the cinematography for Jezebel. The connection between Four Daughters, the 1938 hit in which Garfield achieved stardom in his very first film, and which Epstein wrote and Curtiz directed, and Daughters Courageous, in which Curtiz, Epstein and Garfield are again united, is very close. The cast, which last year was in Four Daughters and this year is in Daughters Courageous, includes Garfield, Priscilla, Lola and Rosemary Lane, Gale Page, May Robson, Jeffrey Lynn, Claude Rains, Frank McHugh and Dick Foran. In addition, Daughters Courageous also has Miss Bainter and Donald Crisp.[17]

The reason Ernest Haller is pointed out as cinematographer is because the credited James Wong Howe fell ill during production and Haller replaced him for the duration of the movie.

Perhaps one of the reasons why Garfield didn't have a larger role in this film despite his popularity and top billing is that they were trying

17 Daughters Courageous Due to Open. *Oakland Tribune.* July 26, 1939

to recreate a similar dynamic to *Four Daughters*, where they establish the conservative family and then throw Garfield's more rebellious character into the mix. His scenes were so good though that it never really felt like he wasn't a big part of the story. Garfield's chemistry with Priscilla Lane again came through in their scenes together, particularly when they first meet, but also in the additional scenes with Claude Rains. It is also commendable that the family dynamic is different in this movie than in *Four Daughters*—instead of a single dad, it was a single mom, and Rains portrayed a completely different sort of father figure. Despite the fact that the cast and crew were exactly the same, it feels like a very different movie overall.

John Garfield and Priscilla Lane were re-teamed in their next film *Dust Be My Destiny* and in the starring roles. The intention, at first, was to cast Ann Sheridan opposite Garfield, then Jane Bryan, and then Gloria Dickson, all of whom were announced in the press in separate articles as the film's leading lady. However, the studio thought the chemistry between Lane and Garfield was stronger and planned to team them in several vehicles for which they had ready properties. While he liked working with Priscilla, John Garfield was becoming a bit perturbed by having to play essentially the same type of character in every movie.

DUST BE MY DESTINY

Directed by Lewis Seiler
Screenplay by Robert Rossen based on the novel by Jerome Odlum
Produced by Hal B. Wallis
Cinematography by James Wong Howe
Edited by Warren Low

Cast:
John Garfield, Priscilla Lane, Alan Hale, Frank McHugh, Billy Halop, Bobby Jordan, Charley Grapewin, Henry Armetta, Stanley Ridges, John Litel, Moroni Olsen, Victor Kilian, Frank Jaquet, Ferike Boros, Marc Lawrence, Arthur Aylesworth, William B Davidson, George Irving, F.W. Jennson, Jack Mower, Edgar Dearing, Sidney Bracey, Creighton Hale, Gertrude Astor, John Hamilton, Ward Bond, Charles Halton, Yakima Canutt, Creighton Hale, Ethan Laidlaw, Lew Harvey George Guhl, Chester Clute, David Kerman, Frank Coghlan Jr, Cliff Clark, Al Herman, William Hopper, Al Harman, Stuart Holmes, Max Hoffman, Jr, Dick Wessle, _Glenn Langan, Anthony Warde, George Offerman jr, Charles Sullivan, Walter Miller, Lee Shumway, George O'Hanlon, John Sheehan, Pat O'Malley, Paul Panzer, Cliff Saum, John J Richardson, Maris Wrixton, Norman Phillips Jr, Garry Owen, Isabel Withers, Tom Wilson.

Released September 16, 1939
Warner Brothers
88 minutes
Black and White

Press accounts promoting *Dust Be My Destiny*, not only announced several different actresses for the leading lady role, they also indicated newcomer Margot Stevenson and veteran Pat O'Brien for roles in the films, and neither appear. An article indicating O'Brien was replaced by Alan Hale is correct, and at the same time announced that Charles Grapewin, John Litel, and Moroni Olsen had been added to the cast. Shortly thereafter, Priscilla Lane was finally announced as John Garfield's leading lady, this time replacing Margot Stevenson, who would later appear with Garfield in *Castle on the Hudson*. Stevenson had apparently settled into the role for a while, with reports of her and Garfield engaging in a torrid love scene for the cameras only half an hour after they first met on the set.

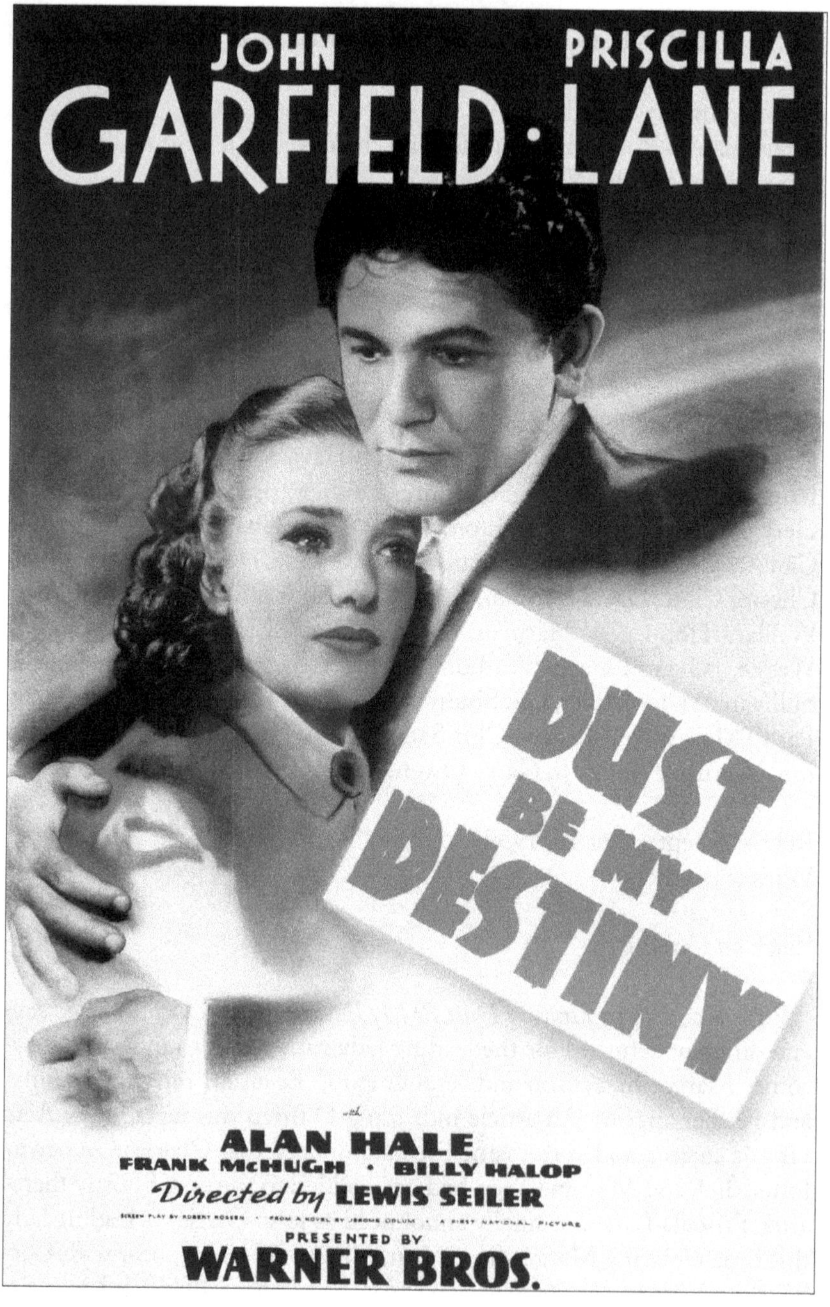

Ad for Dust Be My Destiny.

A bit unsettled with playing essentially the same character, with slight variations, in five out of six movies, Garfield told the press he also worried about "going Hollywood." His misgivings were outlined in an article by Harry Friedman that indicated his continued connection to group theater and the stage:

Born on New York's East Side, poor and struggling most of his life, John Garfield's greatest fear now is that the wealth and fame which films have brought will make him forget his boyhood dreams and ambitions and "go Hollywood." He is not afraid he will begin to high-hat old friends, dress too expensively, live too lavishly or any of the other familiar "going Hollywood" signs. It is more important changes that worry the actor. "I don't want to lose the true values of life," he said. So, he made a resolution to take regular visits to New York to talk shop with friends in his beloved, Group Theater, and to take some acting lessons from the performers who don't earn a fourth of Garfield's salary. His next trip east will be after completing *Dust Be My Destiny*. Another part of his plan to fight that "going Hollywood" feeling was in moving away from his Beverly Hills house to a small place in Hollywood. There, unsurrounded by high-paid film workers, he can get closer to the man in the street, and, he says, live a normal life with his wife, baby and books, and meditations on sociological and artistic subjects.[18]

Dust Be My Destiny also featured one of the oddest audition procedures of any Warner Brothers movie. An article in the Oakland Tribune stated:

What is probably the strangest screen test ever reported in Hollywood was given at Warner Brothers when a group of young actors had to prove they could actually, milk a cow. The studio needed six milkers for scenes 'of *Dust Be My Destiny*. They had to be engaged from the ranks of the Screen Actors' Guild and that complicated matters considerably. Most of the younger generation of Hollywood thespians have grown up under the impression that milk originates in bottles. Nevertheless, the casting office received a large number of affirmative replies from players who were asked if they could milk cows. The only way to prove it was to put the applicants to the test.[19]

---

18 Garfield Fears Fame Will Make Him Forget Dreams. *San Francisco Examiner.* May 21, 1939

19 Cow Milking Actors Rare. *Oakland Tribune.* June 6, 1939

Anthony Warde, Ward Bond, Charles Grapewine, Edgar Dearing, John Garfield, Billy Halop, Bobby Jordan, and Walter Miller is seated facing away in Dust Be My Destiny.

The casting of two Dead End Kids in *Dust Be My Destiny* was part of Warner Brothers' plan to change the young actors from consistently playing hoodlums. Paul Harrison's column explained:

> There are extensive plans for the rehabilitation of the Dead End Kids who will do a right about face in a military school picture. In *Angels Wash their Faces*, they righteously help to scrub up city politics And two of them, Bobby Jordan and Billy Halop, already have sympathetic roles In *Dust Be My Destiny*[20]

Of course the group would splinter into The East Side Kids, The Little Tough Guys, and, finally The Bowery Boys, eventually evolving from slum kids with a humorous edge to young men who played straight comedy.

Once the cast was finalized, work could commence on *Dust Be My Destiny*. And, despite whatever misgivings he might have had, John Garfield turns in yet another remarkable performance, and his chemistry with Priscilla Lane is again discernible.

John Garfield plays Joe Bell who is being released from prison after serving sixteen months because the guilty man confessed. Bell, once a

---

20 Paul Harrison In Hollywood. NEA syndicate. June 23, 1939

good Samaritan who was caught and falsely accused because he stopped to help a wounded man, is now coarse and bitter, trusting nobody. He and a couple of young friends (Billy Halop and Bobby Jordan) hop a train and are met by two men who have committed a robbery and murder. The men start trouble, and a fight erupts. When they are all caught, the murderers claim that Joe and his friends were in on their crime, and they are sentenced to a work farm. While there, he gets involved with the foreman's stepdaughter, Mabel (Priscilla Lane). The foreman (Stanley Ridges) becomes violent with Mabel, Joe steps in and another fight erupts. Joe runs away, the foreman chases after him, and drops dead of a heart attack. Joe and Mabel run away, but news reports indicate they murdered the foreman and are wanted. They marry, try to flee, and end up working for Nick, a kindly diner owner (Henry Armetta), but the cops catch up with them. Mabel is found at their apartment and is jailed. Joe goes to the jail with a camera, pretending to be a reporter, pulls a gun, and helps Mabel escape. Nick drives them to the train station and they flee again. Settling down once again, Joe tries to get a job as a news photographer. He has no luck until he is in the right place at the right time and gets photos of a bank robbery. This gets him a job on a newspaper run by Mike Leonard (Alan Hale). When gangsters threaten Mike, Joe saves him, but his

Garry Owen offers a free bottle of milk to John Garfield and Priscilla Lane in Dust Be My Destiny.

own picture ends up on the front page, so he tells Mabel they must flee again. She turns him in to the police, believing that a trial will prove him innocent of all crimes. Joe, however, is upset because his continued bitterness won't allow him to trust such circumstance. He seems to be right, as the trial does not go in his favor. Finally, Mabel takes the stand and her impassioned pleas and explanations convince the jury in Joe's favor.

Robert Rossen wrote the screenplay for *Dust Be My Destiny*, and that is what attracted John Garfield to yet another role where he plays an angry young man with a chip on his shoulder. Rossen's script keeps the central character consistent while consistently changing the setting. First, Joe Bell is being released from prison after serving time on a bum rap. This is the catalyst for his bitter mistrust. Even as he encounters kind people, he remains suspicious. Then he hops a train with two young co-horts and gets yet another bad break when implicated in yet another crime he did not commit. This is what places him on a work farm. Out of his element, city boy Joe Bell has trouble milking a cow, and reacts negatively to Mabel, the foreman's stepdaughter, chiding him. This places him on the rockpile, another bad break. When Mabel intercedes, he gets the cushy detail of driving the supervising warden around, this good break is obliterated by yet another bad break when he and Mabel are confronted by the foreman, he ends up dead, and they are believed to have done it.

John Garfield and Priscilla Lane work in a diner while hiding out in Dust Be My Destiny.

Throughout the film, every time things start to look ok and Joe is aided by the kindly Italian diner owner, or the benevolent newspaper editor, a bad break knocks him back down.

Throughout all of this Joe Bell responds to his surroundings. He will briefly be happy and secure in his world, and then be forced to fall back on his bitterly suspicious nature. The good man lurking beneath the surface is being led by the angry man who served over a year in jail for no reason. This is one of the strongest elements of this movie, the cyclical nature of good things followed by bad things, and Joe's unwillingness to entertain the idea that there are good people in the world who genuinely want to help him, despite the wrong that has been done to him in the past.

A highlight is when, in a moment, of desperation Joe takes a gun and goes to a store with the intention of robbing it. Instead, he is greeted by an elderly shopkeeper who immediately figures out that he doesn't have any money to pay for anything and tells him he can pay her back later, while offering him food and coffee. Joe doesn't say a word during this exchange, but the look on his face is one of confusion that someone would be so kind to a stranger, and he is clearly torn as to what to do. He ends up leaving the store and not committing the planned robbery.

And while Garfield again has great chemistry with Priscilla Lane, this film is different in that it gives their characters more time to settle into their relationship, and they go through so many ups and downs together. There is a telling scene where Mabel decides to leave Joe while they are on the road, but as they are walking away from each other, they keep turning back to look at the other person, before Mabel finally runs back to him.

Robert Rossen's original script had Joe and Mabel being shot to death, but the downbeat ending played badly with preview audiences. Rossen was told to write a happy ending, which would later be filmed and used for the movie's general release. Rossen refused. Seton I. Miller wrote the ending, and Garfield, who sided with Rossen, protested having to film it.

John Garfield was able to convey a believable performance as a man whose means of transportation was hopping trains, as Garfield himself did much of that before entering films. At one point while filming on location, Billy Halop fell on the tracks in front of an oncoming train, and Bobby Jordan pulled him away just in time, saving his life. Garfield saw many such situations in his railroading days, and they didn't usually end well. This incident with his two fellow actors shook him up considerably and he stopped working for that day.

Critics were pleased with *Dust Be My Destiny* with Paul Walker of *The Harrisburg Telegraph* stating:

Alan Hale congratulates John Garfield and Priscilla Lane in Dust Be My Destiny. *Screenwriter Robert Rossen was not pleased with the happy ending.*

Plot's highly impossible and the apparent facts are subjected to a great deal of dramatization but the fact remains that a motion picture of real entertainment qualities and one that calls attention to an actual situation in this country has been created. John Garfield is already one of the better actors in Hollywood. Priscilla Lane is on the upgrade. Expert characterizations are turned in by Alan Hale, Henry Armetta et al.[21]

21 Walker, Paul. Reviews and Previews. *Harrisburg Telegraph.* September 18, 1939.

Dust Be My Destiny was also a big hit with moviegoers, and another box office hit for John Garfield.

John Garfield was established enough now to challenge the studio's consistently giving him the same type of role. They planned for his next film to be *The Roaring Twenties*, once again with Priscilla Lane, but also featuring James Cagney and Humphrey Bogart. It was a supporting role, but Garfield liked the cast and recognized a good script, so he accepted the role. The studio brass decided it wasn't a big enough role for their new star, and he'd be overshadowed by Cagney and Bogart, so he was replaced by Jeffrey Lynn.

Warner Brothers then wanted John Garfield to next appear with Bogart and George Raft in *Invisible Stripes*, but a still angered Garfield refused, which caused him to be placed on suspension. Allegedly, Garfield, remembered when he was not allowed to play in *Golden Boy* at Columbia and William Holden got the role. He told the studio to get William Holden for *Invisible Stripes* instead. They did.

Warner next offered Garfield a role in a film called *Angels Wash Their Faces* with Ann Sheridan and The Dead End Kids. Believing it might be a sequel to the James Cagney classic *Angels With Dirty Faces*, which also featured Sheridan and the Dead Enders, Garfield agreed to read the script. When he saw it was merely a straight man part to the antics of the Dead End Kids, and not a sequel to the Cagney film at all, but a B movie to star the young actors, he turned it down, telling the studio he would rather remain on suspension and play tennis. Ronald Reagan was cast in the role.

Finally, the studio offered John Garfield the lead in a proposed remake of their 1933 hit *20,000 Years in Sing Sing* which starred Spencer Tracy and Bette Davis. Garfield requested a screening of the earlier film, and after watching it, he told the studio brass that he'd do the remake, but only if they agreed to not change the original ending. They complied, and that became John Garfield's next movie project, under the title *Castle on the Hudson*.

CASTLE ON THE HUDSON

Directed by Anatole Litvak
Screenplay by Seton I. Miller, Brown Holmes, and Courtney Terrett from a book by Lewis Lawes.
Produced by Hal B. Wallis
Cinematography by Arthur Edeson
Edited by Thomas Richards

Cast:
John Garfield, Ann Sheridan, Pat O'Brien, Burgess Meredith, Henry O'Neill, Jerome Cowan, Guinn "Big Boy" Williams, John Litel, Margot Stevenson, Willard Robertson, Edward Pawley, Billy Wayne, Nedda Harrigan, Wade Boteler, Barbara Pepper, Robert Strange, Grant Mitchell, Eddie Acuff, Frank Faylen, Pat Flaherty, Ed Gargan, Howard Hickman Stuart Holmes, James Flavin, Alan Davis, Michael Conroy Brenda Fowler, Sol Gorss, Max Hoffman Jr, Robert Homans, Jay Eaton, Nat Carr, Tom Wilson, Bob Reeves, Emmett Vogan, Dick Wessel, Julie Stevens Ernest Whitman, Thomas Jackson, William Hopper, Eddie Kane, John Lester Johnson, Adrian Morris, Paul Hurst, Ernest Whitman, Cliff Saum, William Telark, Frank Sully, Charles Sherlock, Ernie Adams, Lola Cheany, Willie Keeler, Frank Mayo, Frank Puglia, Max Marx, Mike Lally, John Kelly, Phil Morris.

Released February 17, 1940
Warner Brothers
77 minutes
Black and White

By the time John Garfield agreed to leave his studio suspension and appear in this remake of *20,000 Years in Sing Sing*, he had established a very firm screen persona, mostly created by Warner Brothers based on the roles he'd been playing. When referring to this project as another prison picture, Garfield would quip to the press, "I wish they'd parole me!" While John Garfield was on suspension, the sequel to *Four Daughters*, entitled *Four Wives*, was released. Because Garfield had been the reason for the first film's success, Warners wanted to find a way to use his character despite it having been killed off in the previous movie. Thus, a scene featuring Garfield, was shown in *Four Wives* during a flashback

John Garfield is back in prison in Castle on the Hudson.

sequence. Of course this was a ploy for box office, because the newspaper ads trumpeted John Garfield's name as among the cast, and some theater marquees exhibited "John Garfield in *Four Wives*" despite his having next to nothing to do with the movie.

Garfield's stardom might not have been as comfortable for the serious method actor as a more versatile series of roles might have been, but his old reform school was certainly proud of their alumnus:

> The most prominent alumnus of Angelo Patri's famous school for underprivileged children in New York City has not been forgotten by the new generation of students. John Garfield, star of

Castle on the Hudson, a product of Manhattan's toughest neighborhoods and now one of the bright young "comers" of Hollywood, is the alumnus. Almost daily in his fan mail he receives a gift of some sort from underprivileged youngsters who are now being given the same advantages he received from Patri years ago. The gifts usually take the form of some product from the school's vocational training courses.[22]

John Garfield admitted in interviews that he did have some trepidation doing a role that had once been played by Spencer Tracy, one of the finest actors in motion pictures, and Ann Sheridan echoed similar sentiments about essaying a role that had previously been done by Bette Davis. However, each actor's approach is different than the previous actor who had played the role. Garfield, especially, makes the role his own.

John Garfield plays Tommy Gordon, a cocky crook whose shyster lawyer Crowley (Jerome Cowan) has gotten him out of serving time over several years and many crimes. However, after a bank robbery where a guard is assaulted, Tommy goes to trial, is found guilty, and is sent to Sing Sing Prison. Crowley attempts to make a deal with the prison's Warden (Pat O'Brien), but this fails, as the Warden is serious and doesn't give attention to crooked ward healers. Tommy initially rebels against the prison rules, then realizes life is easier if he plays along, always looking for a chance to escape. That chance happens with a couple other prisoners, including highly intelligent Steve Rockford (Burgess Meredith), but Tommy has a superstition about Saturday being a bad luck day for him, and that's what day it is. He refuses to go along, and there is a gunfight with guards where one prisoner is killed, another is captured, and Rockford jumps to his death. The Warden is impressed with Tommy's refusal to escape, especially after finding his cell door had been unlocked for him to do so. As a result, when word arrives at the prison that Tommy's girl Kay (Ann Sheridan) is near death after a car crash, the Warden allows Tommy a 24 hour parole to see her. When he arrives, she tells him that Crowley had her in a speeding car and attempted to rape her, so she jumped from the vehicle, hence her injuries. When Crowley shows up at the apartment, a fight breaks out with Tommy. Crowley attempts to shoot Tommy, but Kay shoots Crowley first. Tommy escapes, but of course he is accused of the murder and sentenced to the electric chair, even though Kay survived her injuries and insists she was the one who killed Crowley.

Castle on the Hudson is an extremely fast-paced film. Tommy is shown leaving the bank in a getaway car, meeting up with and arriving at a night-

---

22 Garfield Recalled by Successors at Patri School. *Los Angeles Times*. February 20, 1940

Prisoners Burgess Meredith and John Garfield are reminded by Warden Pat O'Brien that there be no talking while working in Castle on the Hudson.

club with Kay, dancing with her, getting arrested, going to trial, and is on his way to prison all in under eight minutes. These are merely establishing scenes from which the narrative builds.

John Garfield's approach to the role of Tommy differs significantly from Spencer Tracy's in the earlier film, despite the movie being a pretty faithful remake of the original. Where Tracy was more aggressive, Garfield plays the character as more pragmatic. In this film, Tommy spits out his angry lines in the manner that Garfield had established as far back as *Four Daughters*, whereas Tracy yelled with passion. Garfield's ability to convey a variety of believable emotions within the same character rivaled Tracy's. Both actors excel equally when they have to switch from unbridled rebellion to crestfallen heartbreak upon hearing of Kay's serious injuries.

Contemporary audiences might find the idea of the Warden letting a prisoner out overnight to be far-fetched, but such programs were a part

John Garfield's devoted girl is Ann Sheridan in Castle on the Hudson.

of the prison system at the time. The only stickler is that the Warden in this film does not appear to have any such progressive ideas. When we are introduced to him and he refuses Crowley's attempt at bribery, we see him as not only honest and clean, but he presents himself as going quite strictly by the book. However, Pat O'Brien is an actor who can effectively anchor each scene with a powerful presence. We believe the Warden's authority as well as his compassion. Tommy has an outlet to escape after the Crowley murder, until he sees a headline that indicates the Warden will be asked to resign for allowing a prisoner probation who is believed to have committed murder. Tommy, having been reformed, returns to turn himself in. But even at the very end, he continues to reaffirm his toughness.

Burgess Meredith plays a convict who is too smart to be in prison, but it is revealed he succumbed to desperation because his wife was having a baby. When he discovers that his intelligence isn't enough to pull off a prison break, he decides that his death is preferable to life in prison. This tragic character augments Garfield's nicely. Guinn "Big Boy" Williams is tragic in another way. He is stereotypically dopey, and when he is ready to go to death row, begs for two more weeks as his prison time has allowed him to learn to play his harmonica better. His weeping refusal to go peacefully to the electric chair is heartbreaking, however it can be argued that Williams, who specialized in these roles, did not match the acting of Warren Hymer in the original. Hymer's vast stage training better informed his performances, and he gave the character more depth and substance. But this scene shows a glimmer of vulnerability in Tommy. Garfield plays the scene quite beautifully, as Tommy watches his fellow inmate break down while being escorted to the electric chair, realizing that will soon be his fate. Garfield keeps his character's face stoic, but with tears visibly forming in his eyes. It is a truly powerful moment that makes the scene.

One can't really make a comparison between Ann Sheridan and Bette Davis in that neither is given enough to do in their respective films. Sheridan comes off just fine, very capable of playing the loyal, tragic, supportive girlfriend. Garfield was quite adept at playing the tough guy who had a tender side when it came to the woman he loved, so their few scenes together are impactful.

Castle on the Hudson was well received, but was not promoted by the studio as a significant production. In many markets, it played at the bottom half of a double bill headlined by the W.C. Fields-Mae West feature *My Little Chickadee*. Despite the Fields-West film being the draw on these double bills, Garfield was satisfied with his work and with the finished film.

John Garfield was not, however, satisfied with Warner Brothers' next assignment for him, a film called *Flight Angels* to be produced by Brian Foy's B-movie unit. Garfield wanted to act in a comedy, telling the studio brass that he excelled in that genre on stage. He also was open to making a romantic drama. The studio suspended him again.

John Garfield had married his wife, Roberta (Robbie) in 1935 and by this time they had a daughter, Katherine, who had been born in 1938. Having struggled in the early years, John and Robbie were financially comfortable by this time, as they did not live extravagantly and put a great deal of John's salary in the bank. Robbie was very supportive of John, and he often told the press she was "my harshest critic." So, when John refused to do roles Warners earmarked for him, suspensions without pay did not hamper them too much financially, and Robbie remained supportive. However, they sometimes believed that the stress of movie making was such that they might have been happier when they had less financially. According to Garfield's biographer, Larry Swindell:

> The work had turned out to be harder than anything he'd expected. He said one thing an actor on the stage knew least about was how grueling a screen actor's life could be, and at Warners very often was. (Joan Blondell once reported that she made 27 films in a 32-month period, six days a week, without any kind

of break). Garfield worked from September, 1938 until August, 1939, without a vacation or even a brief furlough, always on time for the 6:30am call, every day except Sunday. His reward was suspension from salary for refusing to make inferior movies.[23]

Garfield met with Warner producer Henry Blanke, a friend, and was essentially told that because he had firmly established himself as a tough guy, producer Hal Wallis, and studio head Jack Warner were merely trying to protect their investment.

Garfield was finally removed from suspension upon working out a deal for a movie that he found acceptable. According to the press:

> John Garfield, who didn't like his parts, and Warner Bros., who didn't like his attitude, are at peace again. Maybe it's an armed truce, for Garfield walked back onto a sound stage after a three months absence announcing: "If they hand me another stinker, I'll walk out" has been under suspension after turning down parts which the studio selected for him. "But that's all over now," he declared. "I gave In. But they know I want something besides prison pictures. And I still know what I want. Garfield hasn't' played prison pictures, strictly speaking, but his parts have been on the heavy side. Now he wants to do something with comedy, or romance, or both.[24]

The film that Garfield agreed to do was *Saturday's Children*, based on a play by Maxwell Anderson with whom the actor was familiar. Garfield was pleased that the Epstein brothers, Jules and Phillip, would be writing the screenplay, and that Olivia de Havilland would be his co-star. Ms. de Havilland had already been in a Lux Radio Theater version of the play with Robert Taylor a few years earlier and knew the role well. However, what John Garfield was especially pleased about was that *Saturday's Children* was enough of a departure from the roles he had been playing. He wasn't a tough mug from the wrong side of the tracks. He was an honest, hard-working man struggling to survive. This concept appealed to John Garfield on several levels.

---

23 Swindell, Larry. Body and Soul: The Story of John Garfield. NY: Morrow. 1975
24 Garfield Ends Three-Months Balk. *Pomona Progress Bulletin.* January 1, 1940

SATURDAY'S CHILDREN

Directed by Vincent Sherman
Screenplay by Julius J. Epstein and Phillip G. Epstein
Produced by Hal B. Wallis, Henry Blanke
Cinematography by James Wong Howe
Edited by Owen Marks

Cast:
John Garfield, Anne Shirley, Claude Rains, Roscoe Karns, Lee Patrick, Dennie Moore, George Tobias, Elisabeth Risdon, Berton Churchill, Gus Glassmire, Maris Wrixton, Paul Panzer, Jack Mower, Eddie Borden, Jack Wise, Tom Dugan, Lucile Fairbanks, Claude Wisberg, Frank Faylen, John Qualen, Sam Flint, George O'Hanlon, Creighton Hale, Nell O'Day, John Ridgley (voice only), Margot Stevenson (voice only).

Released May 11, 1940
Warner Brothers
102 minutes
Black and White

There was trouble from the outset during the pre-production phase of *Saturday's Children*, which had the working title of *Married, Pretty and Poor*. First, Olivia de Havilland refused to be in the film and was suspended. Louella Parsons reported in her column:

> News was that Warners have suspended Olivia de Havilland, right on the heels of her triumph in *Gone with the Wind*, is this morning's big surprise from Hollywood. The trouble is over Olivia's refusal to return to the coast immediately to play the femme lead in *Married, Pretty and Poor* with John Garfield. Her side of the story is that she has no objection to the script or the role, but she is very tired after making *Gone with the Wind* and *Raffles* and she is going to take a rest suspension or no suspension.[25]

She was replaced by Jane Bryan, an actress with whom John Garfield wanted to work. The young Jane had scored triumphantly in several Warner releases, including *Marked Woman*, *Kid Galahad* and *Invisible Stripes*,

---

25 Parsons, Louella. Olivia Defies Studio Order, Is Suspended. International News Service (syndicated). December 21, 1939

Anne Shirley was borrowed from RKO to appear opposite John Garfield in
Saturday's Children.

a movie John Garfield had turned down. This idea failed when Jane married businessman Justin Dart at the end of 1939 and decided, after completing her scenes in *Brother Rat and a Baby* (1940) to leave acting all together, breaking her contract with the studio. This almost curtailed the project all together, but then plans were to cast a newcomer, 18-year-old Marilyn Merrick. Instead, Marilyn (usually cast as Lyn Merrick) ended up in *Flight Angels*, another movie John Garfield turned down. There was some discussion of Priscilla Lane taking the role, but Warner Brothers believed that her popularity was on the wane, so the studio decided to go in another direction with her career.

Claude Rains once again plays John Garfield's father-in-law, with Anne Shirley as his daughter, in Saturday's Children.

Finally, Anne Shirley was borrowed from RKO to play the role, at John Garfield's suggestion. She and Garfield had known each other socially and connected with their shared liberal politics. Anne Shirley had won a Best Supporting Actress Oscar for *Stella Dallas* (1937), but RKO was having trouble finding the right property for her. After the surprise hit *Sorority House* (1939), which was followed by another box office hit, *Vigil in the Night* (1940), Shirley's career was on an upswing when she was cast in *Saturday's Children.*

Along with the casting of Anne Shirley, Garfield lobbied to get Vincent Sherman hired as the film's director. Sherman had been an actor friend during Garfield's theater days, and had been working for a couple of years as a dialog director at Warner Brothers. Sherman worked with Humphrey Bogart on two films – *Crime School* and *King of the Underworld* – and his prowess on those two films impressed Bogie to where he requested that Sherman be given a chance to helm *Return of Doctor X*, a B-movie the actor did not want to do. Under Sherman's guidance, a possible wrongheaded production turned out to be a sleeper hit. So, it wasn't too difficult for Garfield to secure his services for *Saturday's Children*, especially after the Epstein brothers supported this request.

John Garfield plays Rims Rosson, an idealistic dreamer who comes up with crafty inventions that are limited in their convenience, but oddly creative in their own way. He works in the offices of a firm that also employs Bobby Halevy (Anne Shirley) and her dad (Claude Rains). None of them are executives, all are struggling, but Rims has the idea to turn hemp into silk, and plans to take a job in Manila to work on that project. He and Bobby fall in love, and he holds off on his plan to marry her. They struggle worse than ever, with cramped living quarters and other limitations. Their love continues in spite of their struggle, but when Bobby is laid off and Rims has to take a cut in pay, they can't earn enough to maintain even their limited lifestyle. They plan to move in with Bobby's parents, even though her sister and brother-in-law (Lee Patrick and Roscoe Karns) also live there. Rims even quips, "six people with one bathroom, we'll need ration cards to use it!" Desperate, Rims looks into the Manila job to see if it is still available to him, and receives a letter, which Bobby opens, stating that it is, but they don't have enough money to also include his wife. Fearing Rims would leave her, Bobby tears up the letter. Feeling guilty, she confesses to Rims what she did, and that she tricked him into marriage so he wouldn't leave for the Philippines in the first place. Upset, he leaves her and moves into a hotel. Her father, desperate for them to stay together, tries to kill himself at work by going into a faulty elevator, so that they can collect on his life insurance. When he only sustains minor injuries, the couple decide to remain together, realizing that despite their struggles, they are still in love. It is then that Bobby tells Rims she is pregnant.

John Garfield would long remember what a pleasurable experience it was to work on *Saturday's Children*, a project where everything went his way. He got the co-stars he wanted, he was working with a playwright and screenwriters he admired, and he got to play a role that is far different than found in any of his previous movies. Rims is honest, earnest, clean-living, upright, enterprising, and creative. He has ideas with no outlet, but he doesn't succumb to bitterness and consider resorting to crime. He remains affable, even when expressing disgust at his status in life. At one point he says, "When I was single, I paid all of my bills on time. Now that I'm married, I'm always broke!" One could even call his character a bit nerdy, particularly toward the beginning of the film, and Garfield is convincing as an inventor eager about his work but also eager to get to know Bobby.

Because director Sherman had a background in method acting, he worked with Garfield to break down the Rims character carefully and supported his approach to the role. It is impressive to see Garfield wearing glasses, smoking a pipe, and responding to situations with "boy oh boy,"

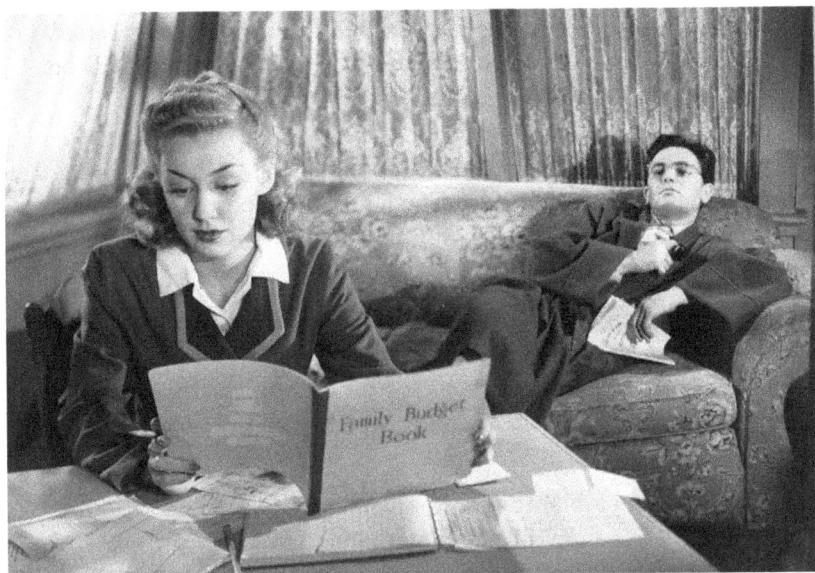

Anne Shirley and John Garfield struggle to make ends meet in Saturday's Children.

rather than bitterly spitting out his lines. Anne Shirley adds the necessary energy and emotion to her role, exhibiting a woman's status in post-Depression/pre-war America, where marriage is her goal, not a career. Lee Patrick and Roscoe Karns are there for laughs, while Claude Rains once again exhibits a commanding presence that anchors the narrative. Elizabeth Risdon, with little screen time, still resonates as Bobby's ditzy mom, as do office workers played by Dennie Moore and George Tobias.

It appears Bobby wants marriage, but it isn't necessarily a priority at first. She is eager to start her job and seems to take pride in her work, and when she is laid off later on because she is married with a working husband, she is clearly very hurt. This film did a good job depicting women in the workplace. Bobby's relationship with her more worldly older sister was also an interesting component to her character, as well as her nice father/daughther moments with Rains, and the film did a good job with the transition from light and romantic prior to Bobby and Rims' marriage to darker and more dramatic afterward.

The May 4, 1940 issue of the Hollywood trade magazine *Showmen's Trade Review* offered tips for exhibitors to promote *Saturday's Children*, emphasizing the fact that John Garfield was playing a much different type of role:

> Perhaps the most significant aspect in connection with *Saturday's Children* is the fact that John Garfield has a role differ-

ent from any other he has ever enacted during the screen career. According to the publicity, "Garfield laughs," and that will be welcome news to moviegoers. The picture also has a story that's bound to hit home for it concerns the struggles of a young couple during their first year of married life. Besides an intriguing title, there arefour names which should be responsible for much activity at the box office – John Garfield, Anne Shirley, Claude Rains, and Roscoe Karns.[26]

Saturday's Children was a pleasant film with likeable characters to which period moviegoers could relate. As a result, it was well received and John Garfield was gratified to have a successful film in which he didn't play a hood. The critics were also pleased, with Bosley Crowther of *The New York Times* stating:

> No studio in Hollywood seems to have a more consistent regard for the American middle class, with its myriad little sorrows and triumphs, its domestic delights and dissensions, than Warner Brothers, whose latest compliment to the proud but hard-pressed poor is paid in *Saturday's Children,*a gently humored and deeply affectionate screen treatment of Maxwell Anderson's memorable tragi-comedy of the same title. All the bitter-sweet essence of that little play, all the tiny torment of its two young married lovers in their baffling conflict with the economic law, is appealingly captured in this third-time remake, which has the further advantage of some deliciously comic byplay. Considering the number of times lately that the screen has been burdened with the story of the young couple, "white collar" workers in New York, who marry, quarrel and make up, it is all the more gratifying that the Warners—and Director Vincent Sherman—have been able to give it a vitality and freshness which make it seem almost new. Particular praise is in store for John Garfield, the sallow Romeo with the sad face and troubled soul, who falls into the part of the harassed young lover as though it had been written for him alone, and to Anne Shirley, who endows the little wife with heroic integrity and strength of character.[27]

Film Daily agreed in their April 17, 1940 review, which stated:

> This picture is genuine entertainment in every respect. Telling a story of young love and its customary troubles, the film is entirely human and honest with a strong appeal, as it doubtless

---

26 Saturday's Children. *Showmen's Trade Review.* May 4, 1940
27 Crowther, Bosley. Saturday's Children review. *The New York Times.* May 4, 1940

has its counterpart many thousands of times over. Nothing has been done to give it a fairy story ending, preserving its honesty with rare fidelity of plot. Exhibitors will find a wealth material in the names in the cast and the opportunities offered by the story itself for a thorough exploitation job, and the picture should appeal to audiences generally. The players are sincere and moving in their performances with no weak sisters in the entire cast.[28]

However, exhibitors complained in the trades that while the movie did draw a decent audience, the moviegoers were displeased with the film. In *Box Office* a theater owner stated: "Insipid. It's a shame to waste John Garfield in a show like this. Drew a fair crowd but did not please too well." Meanwhile, in *Motion Picture Herald*, another theater owner warned: "This picture talked the audience to boredom. All dialog and no action, not even relieved by some little humor. The kind of a picture that the audience fidgets waiting for something to happen and then wonders why they ever came. So did I."

Despite exhibitor complaints, the box office returns were good, and thus Warner Brothers was pleased with the success of *Saturday's Children*. John Garfield was under the impression that the studio would then give him the chance to branch out and play different types of roles in his subsequent movies. This seemed like the direction the studio might go, when Garfield was told that Warner Brothers planned a big production as his next film. Unfortunately, when he was first given the script, Garfield discovered he'd be cast as a hood on the run in that film. He also balked at the idea that the movie was a "big production," in that it was being produced for Bryan Foy's B-movie unit. However, upon reading the script, John Garfield realized the character he'd be playing would not be the same as those he'd done in the type of films he wanted to get away from. This character was more layered and complex, and would allow his acting skills to build upon the base persona he had established and expand his performance according to the depth of the character. John Garfield agreed to do *Flowing Gold* as his next release.

---

28 Saturday's Children review. *Film Daily*. April 17, 1940

FLOWING GOLD

Directed by Alfred E Green
Screenplay by Keith Gamut based on a story by Rex Beach
Produced by William Jacobs
Cinematography by Sid Hickox
Edited by James Gibbon

Cast:
John Garfield, Frances Farmer, Pat O'Brien, Raymond Walburn, Cliff Edwards, Tom Kennedy, Granville Bates, Jody Gilbert, Edward Pawley, Frank Mayo, William Marshall, Sol Gorss, Virginia Sale, John Alexander, E.E. Clive, Russell Wade, Robert Elliot, Eddie Acuff, Eily Malyon, Erville Anderson, Stuart Holmes, Lee Phelps, Al Bridge, Dutch Hendrian, Frank O'Connor, Glen Cavender, George Haywood, Eddy Chandler, Stuart Holmes, Sailor Vincent, Cliff Clark, William Haade, G. Pat Collins, Phyllis Godfrey, Heinie Conklin, William Gould, Phillip Morris, Dick Wessell, Jack Mower.

Released August 4, 1940
Warner Brothers
81 minutes
Black and White

As *Flowing Gold* was taking shape, there were various press reports regarding the cast, director, and screenwriter that seemed to fluctuate with various negotiations. In February of 1940, this announcement hit the press:

> Wayne Morris, who took time off to fly east last week to attend "*The Fighting 69th*" dinner in New York, arrived back in Hollywood to discover that Warner Bros, have plans to put him into the Rex Beach oil field narrative, *Flowing Gold*. It will be a hemannish role for Wayne and follows his appearance in *Double Alibi*, which he did on loan to Universal with Margaret Lindsay. Morris was most recently in *Brother Rat and a Baby*. Tom Reed is writing the screenplay for *Flowing Gold* and Lewis Seiler will direct.

John Garfield starred in Flowing Gold.

Neither Morris, Seiler, nor Tom Reed were active on the project once it began production.

The next announcement seemed rather promising regarding the caliber of director that was sought for the project:

> Raoul Walsh will be the director of *Flowing Gold*, an oil field story written by Rex Beach. Frances Farmer is sought as the lead in the picture, because a vigorous feminine type is needed. Miss Farmer has been working in *South of Pago Pago*.

In fact, it was John Garfield who recommended Frances Farmer for the female lead after both Ann Sheridan and Olivia de Havilland passed on the project. He was friends with Farmer socially, had known her in his theater days, and hoped that a good performance in this film would secure her a Warner contract.

It is unfortunate Raoul Walsh didn't remain with the project. He had just directed *The Roaring Twenties* (1939) for Warner Brothers, and then went over to Republic Pictures to helm *Dark Command* (1940), which became a hit for John Wayne, who was then building his career. But the studio instead assigned him to *They Drive By Night* (1940) which was the project Ann Sheridan also opted for. It also starred George Raft, Humphrey Bogart, and Ida Lupino.

The choice of Alfred E. Green as director was still a competent one. Green had been active since the early silent movie era, helming films with the likes of Jack Pickford and Thomas Meighan. He had just finished directing *South of Pago Pago*, which was a successful project for Frances Farmer. Thus, he knew how to successfully work with the sometimes unpredictable actress, so with both his guidance and Garfield's friendship, Warner Brothers were willing to hire her for *Flowing Gold*.

John Garfield plays John Alexander, an oilfield worker who is on the lam from a murder rap, and going by Johnny Blake. Pat O'Brien is Hap O'Connor, who is familiar with Johnny's wanted poster because police have been looking for him, but decides to hire him on to replace an irresponsible worker who has been drinking on the job. When the disgruntled employee prepares to attack Hap, Johnny stops him and knocks him out after a scuffle. Hap feels obligated to Johnny and protects him, even after he has designs on Linda (Frances Farmer) whom Hap is also fond of. She is the daughter of Wildcat Chalmers (Raymond Walburn), owner of the well that Hap's crew, including Johnny, are currently digging. When Johnny is jailed after a brawl and his fingerprints are taken, he realizes it is only a matter of time before the law realizes who he is, so he decides to leave. Hap breaks his leg in an accident, so Johnny stays and helps bring in the well. When he and Linda admit they are in love, Johnny comes clean and reveals he killed a man in self-defense and is wanted. When lightning hits their well and sets it on fire, Johnny helps Hap and the crew put the fire out, even though the sheriff is there to arrest him. When they put the fire out, Johnny goes peacefully with the law and Linda joins him. They are confident he will beat the charge in court.

Flowing Gold is aggressive like a B-level movie, with rousing action sequences, but it is mounted like an A-level movie, with a top cast, a good director and some impressive effects with gushing oil wells, and such.

And the character John Garfield plays is once again a tough guy who spits out his dialog in short bursts, but he is not a hood, as we discover early in the film. In fact, *Flowing Gold* jumps right into Garfield's character traits. Johnny is seen waiting with others for an oil rig job site to open, which won't be until the following morning. When he is asked where he's from in casual conversation, he becomes reticent about divulging info, and threatening toward the man who asked. When morning comes and the place opens up, the arrival of two lawmen forces Johnny, who is first in line, to run away.

This opening draws us into the film quickly, causing us to wonder about the character's backstory. We eventually find out that Johnny acted in self-defense and didn't trust the judicial system. And we discover this shortly after he makes a heroic gesture by thwarting an attack on Hap by the discharged alcoholic worker.

John Garfield is able to imbue Johnny with more than just his tough guy traits. He can exhibit sensitivity and vulnerability as well. His first meeting with Linda finds her car stuck in the mud. Johnny's figures out a simple way to extricate her. His wise cracking manner is originally off-putting to Linda, but it eventually wins her over after she gets to know him better. This shows Johnny to be a good guy with a tough manner, not a hood whose environment resulted in a life of crime. Johnny has skills,

John Garfield and Pat O'Brien vie for the attention of Frances Farmer in
Flowing Gold

wants to work, and is willing to work hard. His innate leadership abilities are used to do what is best for his job.

Frances Farmer is exceptionally good as Linda, offering a solid, believable performance. Garfield hoped that Warner Brothers would give her a contract, but she recently had to leave a stage adaption of a Hemingway story because of her erratic behavior. Despite her good work in this movie, the studio didn't want to take a chance. Farmer spent much of the subsequent 1940s offscreen, including time in a mental institution, before returning to acting in the 1950s. She did some random movies and television, including hosting her own TV show, but concentrated mostly on working in stage productions until her death in 1970. Biographies on her, including the famous film with Jessica Lange, have been called inaccurate.

Pat O'Brien is quite good as Hap, using his uncanny ability to portray a fast-talking tough guy and a soft-spoken man of understanding and reason, all within the same character. This made him especially good at playing authority figures like the warden in *Castle on the Hudson*, or, maybe most famously, the Priest in *Angels With Dirty Faces* (1938) opposite his friend James Cagney.

It is an interesting idea to fill out the cast with actors who do comedy, such as Raymond Walburn as Wildcat, burly Tom Kennedy as the ironically nicknamed Petunia, and Cliff Edwards who has a chance to do a couple of comedy bits with his ukulele. Kennedy was a long time veteran of screen comedy, having started in Mack Sennett's Keystone comedies during the silent movie era. He essays a character role well, filling it out with both dramatic scenes and more lighthearted ones.

Cliff Edwards was delightfully quirky with Buster Keaton in the MGM early talkies *Doughboys* (1930) and *Sidewalks of New York* (1931), and had evolved into a solid character actor with appearances in films like *His Girl Friday* (1940), and even made an appearance in *Gone With The Wind* (1939). When he appeared in *Flowing Gold* he had already provided the voice of Walt Disney's Jiminy Cricket in *Pinocchio* (1940), and would do so in a series of animated shorts during the 1950s. The comedy relief he supplies in *Flowing Gold* is augmented by heavyset Jody Gilbert as his wife.

Raymond Walburn's croaking voice was a mainstay in movies at this time, adding his bluster to everything from Frank Capra's *Mr Deeds Goes to Town* (1936) to the John Wayne western *Dark Command* (1940).

Flowing Gold enjoyed a significant amount of success, and John Garfield helped promote it when he guest-wrote Walter Winchell's column on one of the days during Winchell's August vacation (it was likely penned by a ghost writer with Garfield's byline). Still, of the film, he stated:

William Marshall, Tom Kennedy, Cliff Edwards, Pat O'Brien, Frances Farmer, John Garfield in Flowing Gold.

Before I played in *Flowing Gold,* all I knew about oil was that the East river, where I swam as a kid in New York, was messy with it and that I got plenty on the seat of my pants sliding to second on the tenement streets. Discovery of oil played the same pranks on men's lives as the discovery of gold. Towns sprang into existence overnight, and fortunes were grabbed and spent recklessly. Most of us are less familiar with the story of oil than with that of gold, but its lore is as rich and colorful.[29]

However, despite the success of *Flowing Gold,* John Garfield was dissatisfied with next being cast in a movie that James Cagney turned down. Cagney was also growing tired of playing hoods, having just enjoyed success as a gangster in Raoul Walsh's *The Roaring Twenties* (1939). So the year 1940 saw Cagney venture into different roles, such as a cowardly soldier in *The Fighting 69th* or the boxer who is blinded in the ring in *City for Conquest.* It is not surprising that Cagney didn't want to do *East of the River.* The film's plot has the same dynamic as his 1938 success *Angels With Dirty Faces.*

---

29 Walter Winchell On Broadway. *New York Daily Mirror.* December 2, 1940.

Warner Brothers liked the concept of two friends connected with each other since childhood, where one is an all-around good guy, who attends school and works hard, while the other is a delinquent who does time in prison and comes out a racketeer but with redeeming qualities that the narrative reveals. John Garfield felt, and correctly so, that this idea had become cliched. Even before *Angels With Dirty Faces*, the idea had been utilized by MGM for William Powell and Clark Gable in *Manhattan Melodrama* (1934).

Despite his misgivings, John Garfield's next movie was another in which he was cast as a hood. However, because the character had redeeming values, and a backstory that made his status acceptable, Garfield felt that this might be another opportunity to explore his established screen persona's complexities. As a result, he decided to do what he could with *East of the River*.

EAST OF THE RIVER

Directed by Alfred E Green
Screenplay by Fred Niblo based on the story *Mama Ravioli* by Joe Fante and Ross Wills
Produced by Bryan Foy
Cinematography by Sid Hickox
Edited by Thomas Pratt

Cast:
John Garfield, Brenda Marshall, Marjorie Rambeau, George Tobias, William Lundigan, Moroni Olsen, Douglas Fowley, Jack La Rue, Jack Carr, Paul Guilfoyle, Russell Hicks, Charley Foy, Ralph Volkie, Jimmy O'Gatty, Robert Homans, Joe Conti, O'Neill Nolan, Ann Edmunds, Frank Faylen, George Lloyd, William Pawley, Curly Wright, Murray Alper, William Marshall, Roy Barcroft, Jerry Mandy, Eddy Chandle, George Humbert, Richard Clayton, Al Herman, Edward Fielding, Arch Hendricks, Sol Gorss, Creighton Hail, Fred Graham, Frank Mayo, Edwin Stanley, Howard Mitchell, Cliff Saum, Jack Mower, Hector Sarno, Ralph Sanford, Pat O'Malley, Al Rhein.

Released November 9, 1940
Warner Brothers
74 minutes
Black and White

John Garfield's disinterest in playing in yet another programmer for the Warner Brothers B unit was improved when the studio offered him a new contract. According to the press:

> John Garfield has a new contract with Warners that will permit him to do four stage plays during the next six years. In all probability he will make his start under Oscar Serlin's banners. Serlin is the man who produced the enormously successful *Life With Father* in *Nijinsky*, a dramatic story of the dancer which Clifford Odets is to write. Odets' got the Nijinsky idea only to find that Serlin had the rights to the life by Mrs. Eomola Niiinsky. After that they came to an understanding. At the moment, Odets is preparing a film version of *Night Music* in which Garfield appeared in New York; Serlin is trying to get Nijinsky and

his wife into this country and Warners have made their arrangements with the actor, who is preparing to go to work in *East of the River* with Ida Lupino.[30]

Along with announcing Ida Lupino as John Garfield's leading lady, the press also stated that Raoul Walsh was set to direct *East of the River*. However, the studio decided to put Lupino and Walsh on *High Sierra*, which was set to star George Raft. Raft turned the part down because he didn't want to die at the end, so it was given to Humphrey Bogart. Bogart had been appearing in programmers for the most part, unless he had a supporting role. *High Sierra* was such a big hit, it elevated the hard working actor to leading man, and started the journey to his becoming a timeless icon of cinema.

For *East of the River*, Lupino was replaced by Brenda Marshall and the direction was taken over by Alfred E. Green, who had helmed *Flowing*

John Garfield threatens Brenda Marshall in East of the River.

30 Soans, Wood. Six-Year Contract With Warper's Will Allow Four Appearances in *New York. Oakland Tribune.* July 24, 1940

Gold. John Garfield was pleased with Green's direction on the previous film and approved the studio's choice.

John Garfield plays Joe Lorenzo, a criminal who tells his family he is working construction out west. He sends money home to his brother Nick, whom his mother adopted as a child because he was orphaned and homeless. While Joe chose a life of crime, Nick became a successful college student. Joe is framed and sent to San Quentin for a stretch, but keeps corresponding with his family. When he is released, he returns to New York to reconnect with his family, get together with his girl Laurie (Brenda Marshall) and get even with the men who framed him (Douglas Fowley and Jack LaRue). Laurie, a forger, eventually gets caught up in the wholesomeness of Joe's family, including both Nick and their strong, loving Italian mama Teresa Lorenzo (Marjorie Rambeau). Joe sets up a robbery with the men who framed him, then calls the police so they get caught, allowing him to get even. However, while one of them is caught, the other gets away. As a result, Joe has to keep in hiding. Meanwhile, Laurie continues to acclimate into the family and ends up spending a lot of time with Nick, and they fall in love. Joe initially tries to hang on to Laurie with threats, but eventually gives her and Nick his blessing.

East of the River is superficially entertaining, mostly due to John Garfield's strong performance, and the capable contribution of Brenda Marshall, William Lundigan, Douglas Fowley, and Jack LaRue in the supporting roles. Brenda Marshall is a standout as Laurie. She convincingly portrays the transition from tough girl who's been around, to someone who wants the sort of home and family Nick and his mother represent. However, much of the narrative includes Marjorie Rambeau's stereotyped Italian mama, with a broad accent that often seems forced. Rambeau is a fine actress as evidenced by her work in so many other films, but there isn't a lot she can do with this role. Her "at'sa good-a boy!" lines weren't too unusual as to how Italians were depicted in older movies, but it hasn't worn well over time. Yet, somehow, George Tobias playing a similar character doesn't seem as off-putting, probably because it is a much smaller role and it is played for laughs.

There are distinct parallels to *Angels With Dirty Faces* in that the Joe and Nick characters start out as kids that get caught robbing a train car and are about to be sent to reform school. However, in this film, mama intervenes. And while the dynamic of two bad kids growing up to be one good and one bad is standard, the idea that they end up in love with the same woman is even more cliched. As a result, while it is entertaining, and has factors to make it appealing, *East of the River* is the weakest film in which John Garfield has thus far appeared.

A review that appeared in the Hollywood trade magazine *The Movies and the People Who Make Them* stated:

> *East of the River* is a more or less routine but above average Warner Brothers melodrama which makes up for a worn plot by parading considerable cast talent and introducing a few new twists. The major characterizations are well drawn and forceful. John Garfield emerges in a familiar role without straining while William Lundigan shows dramatic instinct. Brenda Marshall maages a convincing metamorphosis from gun moll to nice lady.[31]

However, the fact that *East of the River* was a standard programmer, did not seem to matter with moviegoers. It was another moneymaker for John Garfield, and exhibitors indicated that their patrons were very pleased with it. At least one exhibitor, however, stated in *Motion Picture Herald* that it was "a mistake to use the Italian dialect or brogue. That hurt the picture."

Because it was issued as from Warner's B unit, it was often paired with another movie and held up the bottom half of the double bill (often with the Judy Garland MGM feature *Little Nellie Kelly*). It appears that while Warner Brothers realized that John Garfield was still a moneymaker, and had secured a new contract with him, they planned to spend little on his projects to maximize their profit. They realized that the image that they most closely cultivated for him worked well in the sort of potboiler that was most effectively produced by Bryan Foy and their B unit.

John Garfield's acceptance of *East of the River* was due to the hood having redeeming qualities that extended beyond the usual role. And his contract allowing him to continue his connection to the theater meant that he had an outlet where he could branch out as an actor. But that didn't mean he would simply allow the studio to dictate his projects if he felt they were somehow sub-par.

Although they were content with his appearing in appropriate pro-grammers, Warner Brothers still balked at John Garfield appearing in a supporting part. They were giving him leading man money. But Garfield was happy to play a supporting role when one came along that especially interested him. This happened with *The Sea Wolf*, based on the novel by Jack London.

---

31 East of the River review. *The Movies and the People Who Make Them*. November 9, 1940

THE SEA WOLF

Directed by Michael Curtiz
Screenplay by Robert Rossen based on the novel by Jack London
Produced by Hal Wallis
Cinematography by Sol Polito
Edited by George Amy

Cast:
Edward G. Robinson, John Garfield, Ida Lupino, Alexander Knox, Gene Lockhart, Barry Fitzgerald, Stanley Ridges, David Bruce, Francis McDonald, Howard Da Silva, Frank Lackteen, Cliff Clark, William Gould, Louis Mason, Charles Sullivan, Dutch Hendrian, Eddie Laidlaw, George Magrill, Ernie Adams, Frank Mills, Ralf Harolde, Jeanne Cowan

Released March 2, 1941
Warner Brothers
99 minutes
Black and White

Edward G. Robinson had secured the role of Wolf Larsen for the Warner Brothers' adaption of Jack London's *The Sea Wolf* as early as the Spring of 1940. An article in the press stated:

> Edward G. Robinson received the good news today that his next starring vehicle for Warners will be *The Sea Wolf*. Oldtimers still talk about Hobart Bosworth's masterly portrayal of Wolf Larsen, the brilliant but brutal skipper in Jack London's powerful story. Supporting Eddie will be Olivia De Havilland and Jeffrey Lynn as the young lovers who find themselves virtual prisoners on the cruel sea captain's ship. Lloyd Bacon will direct.[32]

Only months later it was announced that Anatole Litvak would be directing, but it ended up falling into the hands of Michael Curtiz.

Warners had the film rights to the book, which had first been filmed in 1913 by Hobart Bosworth, and then also by Fox in 1930. Screenwriter Robert Rossen split the male romantic lead into two

---

32 Warners Will Star Robinson in Remake of The Sea Wolf. *The San Francisco Examiner.* May 30, 1940

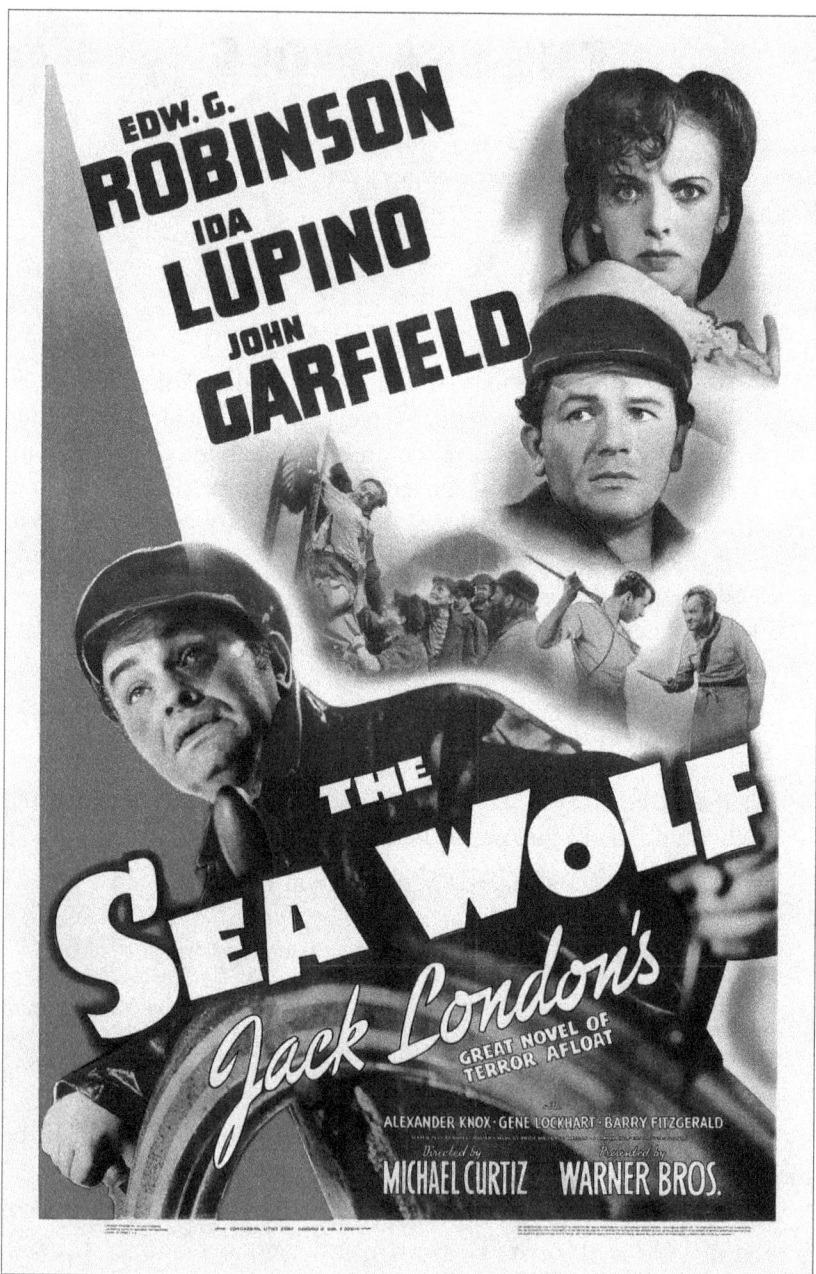

Garfield was billed above the title, but The Sea Wolf *was Edward G. Robinson's movie.*

John Garfield, Ida Lupino, and Edward G Robinson in The Sea Wolf.

parts – an effete literary man, and a rugged criminal on the run from the law. As a result, the casting of the romantic male lead would have to be reassessed and Jeffrey Lynn was no longer attached to the project. While the studio was negotiating with Alexander Knox as the writer, they cast George Raft as the romantic lead.

John Garfield coveted the role Raft was playing in *The Sea Wolf*, as he was a big fan of Jack London's book. Raft was notorious about turning down roles and walking out on productions, sometimes quite famously. He turned down *High Sierra* and *The Maltese Falcon*, both of which became huge hits for Humphrey Bogart, and, as fate would have it, Raft also turned down the role in *The Sea Wolf*, realizing it was Edward G. Robinson's movie. Robinson and Raft had just finished filming *Manpower* (which was released after *The Sea Wolf*) and got along so poorly, they got in an actual fist fight on the set. So, Garfield campaigned for the role. Warners didn't like placing Garfield in supporting roles at leading man pay, but Garfield argued that is exactly what they were planning to do with George Raft. The studio relented and allowed him to take it. Olivia de Havilland also turned down the project, and Ann Sheridan was considered before Ida Lupino was cast. John Garfield was pleased that Michael Curtiz was directing, as he credited Curtiz with helping to make his film debut in *Four Daughters* such a success.

Along with splitting one of the book's characters into two separate roles, Rossen also adapted the screenplay to show Wolf Larsen as more of a tyrant, as well as presenting the philosophical relationship he had with the writer. There were parallels to Hitler, who had come into power as the war in Europe was raging (America would not enter the war until several months after *The Sea Wolf* was released). This aspect of the character is what attracted Robinson, and he offers one of the finest performances of his career.

There isn't a lot for John Garfield to do as the rugged George Leach, and it can be argued that both Alexander Knox's role as the writer, and Ida Lupino's part, enjoyed a larger chunk of the narrative. And, of course, it remained chiefly Edward G. Robinson's movie. But Garfield wanted to be a part of this project and looked forward to supporting Robinson, an actor he liked and respected. By the time filming began, Michael Curtiz was selected as director. And his vision as a filmmaker is one of the reasons why, despite a supporting part, *The Sea Wolf* is one of the best films in which John Garfield appears.

John Garfield plays George Leach, a down on his luck guy who is being sought by police. When it gets difficult to avoid them, he sees an opportunity when a representative from a ship called The Ghost, is trying to hire men as part of its crew. Despite the ship's captain having a reputation as a sadistic tyrant, Leach, who has some experience on a ship, agrees to join the crew, figuring it is better than getting caught by riverfront cops and sent to prison. Writer Humphrey Van Weyden (Alexander Knox) and escaped convict Ruth Webster (Ida Lupino) are on a ferry that is involved in a collision and sinks. They are fished out of the water by The Ghost. Wolf Larsen (Edward G. Robinson) informs Van Weyden that he is to be a part of the crew and lets both know they will not stop at another port. Both are expected to endure the entire trip. When the ship's alcoholic doctor (Gene Lockhart) is humiliated by Larsen one too many times, he climbs to the crow's nest and shouts a lot of revealing information about Larsen, including that he is being hunted by his own brother, who plans to kill him and sink his ship. Leach tries to form a mutiny but it is thwarted and, rather than punish the men, he rewards them, while also revealing that the ship's cook (Barry Fitzgerald) has informed on them. He is thrown overboard, dragged by a rope, and a shark bites off one of his legs. Van Weyden, Leach, and Webster all try to escape with a lifeboat, but discover that Larsen, thinking ahead, filled the water rations with vinegar. Larsen's brother finally catches up with The Ghost and, as it is sinking, Larsen has one of his spells that cause intense headaches and temporary blindness. Van Weyden, Leach, and Webster reboard The Ghost to steal rations, but both men are captured. Van Weyden is shot and tells Larsen he missed and cons him into allowing Leach and Webster to escape. Van Weyden dies and Larsen goes down with his ship.

The character of George Leach was hardly a stretch for John Garfield, and he does have a smaller supporting part. But with Michael Curtiz directing and Edward G. Robinson starring in a film version from a Jack London novel, John Garfield realized his participation in *The Sea Wolf* was still good for his screen career. The film never leaves the studio sound-stage, but it is shot so effectively by Sol Polito and directed so well by Curtiz, one would think they were actually out to sea. According to Alan K. Rode's biography of Michael Curtiz:

> The shots of the ship in motion are silently sepulchral. Byron Haskin's superb miniatures – he was nominated for a special effects Oscar – are complimented by the 130-foot long, 32-foot wide set of The Ghost, assembled by a team of 75 carpenters on Stage 21.[33]

The actors were all skilled and accomplished, so there was little trouble, even with Curtiz's direction. Curtiz was a fine director, but often difficult on the set. Columnist Ward Soans visited the set and recalled:

> When Michael Curtiz is directing a picture, the press agents can sit back and take it easy for what with Curtiz inability to cope with the English language and his fine sense of frenzy in achiev-ing contretemps, it is merely necessary to report the goings on and still get "copy." Take a recent day when Curtiz was engaged in the filming The Sea Wolf. Comes a scene in which John Gar-field is supposed to hurl something at Edward G. Robinson, who dodged at just the right second according to the script; This," decreed Director Curtiz, "is a hard scene. Too many rehearsals will wear you out. The timing must be perfect. We take it once." Robinson interrupted: "How about a few rehearsals? Suppose I don't dodge at the right moment." "Then we take it again," Curtiz sighed. "Film is cheap." They took it once and Robinson, with just the proper shade of alarm in his off eye, dodged the missile. Curtiz had the effect he wanted.[34]

The Sea Wolf held two premieres, one on land and another out to sea, according to press reports:

> *The Sea Wolf,* Warner Brothers' new remake of the Jack London story, will have a double premiere next Friday one at sea, aboard

33 Rode, Alan K. *Michael Curtiz: A Life in Film.* University Press of Kentucky, 2017
34 Ward Soans Column. *Oakland Tribune.* January 16, 1941

John Garfield, Ida Lupino, and Edward G Robinson worked well together in
The Sea Wolf *but not all of them got along.*

the star-studded steamship America, and the other at the Fox
here. Edward G. Robinson, Ida Lupino, John Garfield and many
other stars will view the film at sea. They will disembark here Saturday and motor to a barbecue at London's ranch near Sonoma.[35]

John Garfield's intuition paid off. *The Sea Wolf* was an enormous success,
its box office almost doubling its production costs.

When the film was re-released in 1947 in a double bill with a re-release
of *The Sea Hawk*, both films were trimmed in order to fit comfortably
together on the program. The missing footage for *The Sea Hawk* was
eventually found, but this was not so easy with *The Sea Wolf*. Warner
Brothers edited the original camera negative and discarded the footage.
Warner Archive's George Feltenstein told Leonard Maltin:

> We thought there was no extant 35mm material and John
> Garfield's 16mm print from NYU would be our only source to
> complete the film. The Library of Congress (where we have the
> original on deposit) confirmed that the camera neg was indeed
> cut. We thought we would have to use the 16mm material to
> cut back and forth with the existing short version to get to 100

---

35 Double Premier for Sea Wolf. *San Francisco Examiner.* March 15, 1941.

minutes and the differences would be very noticeable and disappointing. I noticed that we had two fine-grain master positives at MoMA (The Museum of Modern Art). They had been there for 30+ years. Thankfully, I had one of the nitrate fine-grains from MoMA brought here to Warner Bros, just on the off-chance it was complete. When the element arrived it turned out to be a great nitrate fine grain of the original release version. That meant we could not only present the film all from 35mm, but from a 2nd generation nitrate made off the camera negative in 1941. A lot of painstaking cleanup of picture and sound was required. It is somewhat of a miracle as we had given up all hope, but now it's preserved. We released it on DVD as well as Blu-ray since many people still haven't made the leap. The complete version with the additional 13 minutes added heft to several of the scenes between Wolf Larsen (Edward G.) and Van Weyden (Alexander Knox). The pursuit of Larsen and his vessel The Ghost by his brother in another ship also was addressed. In the cut version, this important plot aspect was barely mentioned. Hal Wallis disliked the 'philosophical' interpretation of Wolf Larsen by Robinson and urged Curtiz to curtail this aspect and make Larsen meaner and more sadistic. He also told Curtiz that some of Robinson's line readings sounded too 'New Yorky.' As usual, Curtiz paid his producer lip service, then ignored him and did what he wanted with the film.[36]

Film historian Farran Nehme found greater insight in the newly restored film, stating:

> ...this counts as an entirely different film. The Sea Wolf is an intense anti-Fascist allegory (via then-Communist screenwriter Robert Rossen), and like other such films from its era, feels newly and agonizingly relevant.[37]

John Garfield got along well with Edward G. Robinson and with Ida Lupino, and while Ida liked Garfield, she did not like Robinson. However, this does not show up in their work. And the carefully cast Barry Fitzgerald and Gene Lockhart further enhance the narrative.

Film Daily stated that The Sea Wolf was "Powerful, hard-hitting," and "splendidly cast."[38] Motion Picture Daily called the film "a compelling,

36   The Sea Wolf: Longer and Better. Leonard Maltin's Movie Crazy. October 25, 2017
37   Self Styled Siren: The Year in Old Movies by Farran Nehme. December 29, 2018
38   Sea Wolf review. Film Daily. March 24, 1941

sharply etched drama in which interest never lags, and which carries an emotional impact which should turn it into box office dollars."[39]

John Garfield was co-starred again with Ida Lupino in his next film *Out of the Fog*. In that film, Garfield played the most ruthless character of his entire screen career.

---

39 Sea Wolf review. *Motion Picture Daily.* March 24, 1941

OUT OF THE FOG

Directed by Anatole Litvak
Screenplay by Robert Rossen, Jerry Wald, Richard Macaulay based on the play *The Gentle People* by Irwin Shaw.
Produced by Hal Wallis
Cinematography by James Wong Howe
Edited by Warren Low

Cast:
John Garfield, Ida Lupino, Thomas Mitchell, Eddie Albert, George Tobias, John Qualen, Aline MacMahon, Jerome Cowan, Odette Myrtil, Leo Gorcey, Robert Homans, Bernard Gorcey, Paul Harvey, Frank Darien, Konstantin Sankar, Walter Tetley, Billy Wayne, Charles Drake, Eddie Graham, Richard Kipling, Frank Mayor, Alexander Leftwich, Jack Wise, Murray Alper, Frank Coghlan Jr, Matya Palmera, Jimmy Conlin, Max Hoffman jr, Alec Craig, Herbert Hayood, Frank Darien, Creighton Hale, Jay Eaton, Creighton Hale, Garland Smith.

Released June 14, 1941
Warner Brothers
85 minutes
Black and White

Humphrey Bogart was originally planned as the star of *Out of the Fog* and it was an opportunity for the actor to play a truly despicable character with no redeeming values. He had done this before in films like *Kid Galahad*, but this time he'd have the lead. He liked the idea of the main character being the bad guy all the way through.

However, Ida Lupino, who was already cast and set to receive top billing as the film's star, refused to work with Bogart again. She just finished two movies with him – *They Drive By Night* and *High Sierra* – and found him difficult. At the time, Lupino was a much bigger star than Bogart, whose stardom would just begin to ascend with the success of *High Sierra*. That had not quite happened yet, so Lupino insisted they cast another actor, and suggested John Garfield, with whom she liked working in *The Sea Wolf*. Bogart was incensed by this decision and asked Jack Warner if Ida Lupino was now in charge of the studio's casting department. It all worked out for Bogie. He was put in *The Maltese Falcon*, which helped raise his level of stardom as he headed toward icon status.

John Garfield was also attracted to playing a truly and completely despicable character with no redeeming features in the leading male role. It seemed like something of a challenge for an actor to sustain interest in such a character. There was another factor that attracted John Garfield. *Out of the Fog* was based on Irwin Shaw's play *The Gentle People* which Shaw hoped Garfield would play on stage. He was not available so the stage role went to Franchot Tone. Having the role in the movie felt like redemption.

John Garfield plays Jacob Goff, a cold-hearted schemer who descends upon a small fishing town and demands protection money or he sets boats on fire. He chooses two old men as his victims – Jonah Goodwin (Thomas Mitchell) and Olaf Johnson (John Qualen) – and attempts to shake them down for five dollars per week. A further complication is that Jonah's daughter Stella (Ida Lupino) is tired of the confines of the area where she lives, tired of her affable boyfriend George (Eddie Albert) and is attracted to Goff because of the excitement and underlying danger he exhibits. After Garfield embezzles her father's savings, he talks Stella into running away to Cuba with him. George tries to intervene but is handily beaten up by Goff. Jonah and Olaf offer to take Goff across the sea in their boat to an appointment, with plans to push him overboard. Because they are kindly men, they can't go through with it, but Goff catches them in the act. His reaction causes the boat to rock and he falls overboard and drowns. Detectives investigate, as Goff was a wanted man, but can't find any wrongdoing, so they dismiss the case as an accident. Jonah and Olaf find Goff's wallet, containing their money, and take it back. The cop on the beat sees them, but lets them get away with it.

When screening the preview, critic James Francis Crow was taken aback at how the ending differed from the play (where Jonah and Olaf do go through with their plan to kill Goff). He stated in his article:

> Irwin Shaw's play *The Gentle People* when It was done on the New York stage had a moral in it The moral, as Shaw stated it, went like this: If you want peace and gentleness in this world you have got to take violence out of the hand of violent people and take it into your own hands and use It like a club. Then maybe, Shaw said, on the other side of violence there will be peace and

John Garfield and Ida Lupino were reteamed in Out of the Fog. *Moviegoers didn't like the despicable character Garfield played, although his acting was quite good.*

gentleness. So the two principal characters in Shaw's play a couple of gentle fishermen rise up in wrath against a racketeer who has destroyed their happiness and the happiness of the daughter of one of them and kill him and throw his body in the bay. All of this is changed In the film version written by Robert Rossen, Jerry Wald and Richard Macaulay for the Warner Bros. The moral of *Out of the Fog*, which is the title of the picture adaptation, is somewhat as follows: Just take it easy you gentle people you and be patient and long-suffering and your enemy will accidentally fall out of a boat and be drowned. That is the way it happens in *Out of the Fog* in accordance with The Production Code. It is quite a change indeed from the message that Shaw intended. For a while until the movie writers get in their deadly blows and the Production Code obtrudes itself, *Out of the Fog* is a pretty fair picture. It is somewhat too turgidly melodramatic in the direction by Anatole Litvak and the acting by Ida Lupino, John Garfield. Thomas Mitchell. John Qualen. Eddie Albert. and the others of the east but it is vitally conceived and it retained a firm grip on the preview audience — that is until the boat-rocking sequence. In that particular sequence when the gentle people came at last to deadly grips with their oppressor the audience laughed. Maybe Director Litvak and Scenarists Rossen Wald and Macaulay intended it that way. But I doubt it.[40]

Despite the watering down of the script due to Production Code restrictions in movies at the time, it still has merit, even if Goff's demise feels too convenient and the final scene a bit too light for an otherwise pretty dark story. It's clear throughout the film that Jonah and Olaf are kind men, and it makes sense that they would take the moral high ground and be unable to stoop to Goff's level.

Out of the Fog comes off as a compelling, atmospheric drama that benefits from Anatole Litvak's focused direction and cinematographer James Wong Howe's choice to shoot all of the scenes in soft focus amidst heavy fog, which accentuates the darkness of the situations. The only time the film lights up is in a few cutaway scenes where Goff takes Stella to a bright, noisy nightclub, and a futile attempt by the old men to bring Goff up on charges in court. Both the atmosphere and Garfield's character make this fall under the category of noir.

Garfield turns in one of his finest performances as Goff, a man who describes himself as "filled with rocks" and a product of "the break rods and pool rooms and beer halls and bread lines of the big cities." In his other tough guy portrayals, Garfield spit out his dialog as a rebellious upstart who was a product of his environment and eventually made good. In *Out of the Fog*, Garfield offers a portrayal of relaxed evil, completely confident in who he is and what he's doing. His "full of rocks" character feels nothing for his client victims. If they disrupt his efforts to embezzle, he destroys their property or hurts them (in one jarring scene, Goff beats

---

40   Crow, James Francis. Reviews and Previews. *Los Angeles Evening Citizen News.* June 6, 1941

the elderly Jonah with a rubber hose to teach him a lesson, warning him not to cry out in pain and alert anyone).

Goff capitalizes on Stella's unhappiness and disillusionment, and she responds to the surface without examining the depth. Even when she realizes he is shaking down her father, she continues to see him, perceiving Jonah as a weak man who is browbeaten by her shrewish mother. Goff's callous taking of whatever he desires is the polar opposite of Jonah's passive acceptance. It is an opposite that attracts her, that she perceives as strong and exciting. Garfield and Lupino have extremely strong chemistry in this movie, making it even more believable that Stella would seek Goff's company over someone safer.

Jonah and Olaf's friendship, as portrayed by Mitchell and Qualen, is another example of two actors playing off each other perfectly. Their old-fashioned ways, their kindness and gentleness, are all strong factors in the narrative that offset the despicable actions of Goff. Jonah and Olaf appear to have a very deep familial love for each other, and are the furthest thing from the man who admits he is "filled with rocks" inside.

Unfortunately, despite his fine work as an actor, John Garfield's fans were not pleased with seeing him as a purely despicable character. *Out of The Fog* was not as successful at the box office as the actor's previous films had been. It was a bit too unsettling for audiences and the exhibitors indicated this in the trade magazines: "I'm still in a fog after playing one. Too bad to use such stars in such a picture." "No entertainment value and no luck at the box office. People can get enough gloom from newspapers without paying to see a picture of this type."

Warner Brothers next wanted to John Garfield to appear in *Blues in the Night* once again opposite Priscilla Lane for the first time since *Dust Be My Destiny*. Lane's popularity had since faded and Garfield didn't like the script so he refused to appear. The studio once again put him on suspension before bringing him back for *Dangerously They Live*, a suspense film that intrigued Garfield as something different. However, while on suspension, John Garfield became among the first Hollywood stars to entertain GI troops. It was an experience that would have an even greater impact later on.

DANGEROUSLY THEY LIVE

Directed by Robert Florey
Screenplay by Marion Parsonnet
Produced by Bryan Foy
Cinematography by L. Wm. O'Connell
Edited by Harold McLernon

Cast:
John Garfield, Nancy Coleman, Raymond Massey, Lee Patrick, Moroni Olsen, Esther Dale, John Ridgely, Christian Rub, Frank Reicher, Ben Welden, Cliff Clark, Roland Drew, Arthur Aylesworth, John Harmon, Matthew Boulton, Gavin Muir, Ilka Grüning, Frank M. Thomas, James Seay, Murray Alber, Tod Andrews, Charles Drake, Sol Gorss, Dick Wessell, Lon McCallister, Ann Edmonds, Jack Mower, Eddie Graham, Audra Lindley, Leo White, Paul Panzer, Hans von Morhart, Henry Rowland, Henry Victor, Juanita Stark, Leah Baird, Marijo James, Leslie Denison, Sidney Bracey, William Yetter Sr, Lottie Williams, Joan Winfield, Sven Hugo Borg.

Released December 24, 1941
Warner Brothers
77 minutes
Black and White

John Garfield not only turns in one of his best performances in *Dangerously They Live*, it is one of his best roles in movies thus far. He's not a bad kid from the wrong side of the tracks, and his toughness isn't due to bitterness. He is a heroic leading man within the parameters of a then-topical story that takes issue with some of the free world's most notorious enemies of the period.

The film opens with British intelligence agent Jane Graystone (Nancy Coleman) taking a taxi whose driver is with a German spy ring. He is attempting to abduct her but gets in a car accident in which she is injured and taken to the hospital. She feigns amnesia, so an intern, Dr. Lewis (John Garfield) asks to take the case because it is an area of study for him. Jan confides in Lewis, who is skeptical, believing she might actually have amnesia and fabricating everything. A man named Goodman (Moroni

Nancy Coleman is flanked by John Garfield, Moroni Olsen, and Raymond Massey in Dangerously They Live.

Olsen) comes to visit her claiming to be her father, but Jane tells Lewis he is not. When he shows up with specialist Dr. Ingersoll (Raymond Massey) from whom Lewis once took a class, it becomes more difficult for Lewis to believe Jane. Jane plays along with Goodman and agrees to go to his home, but only if Dr. Lewis continues to treat her. While there, she and Lewis uncover more and more until Lewis is completely convinced, but believes Ingersoll has also been duped. Lewis realizes Ingersoll is in with the spy ring when the two go to the district attorney and Ingersoll arranges to have Lewis committed. While being guarded by one of the spies, Dr. Lewis escapes and gets his gun. He comes in and rescues Jane who has been forced to provide important information about a large convoy. The men are captured, authorities are contacted, and arrangements are made to sink German U-boats.

Although it was a programmer for Bryan Foy's B-movie unit at the studio, *Dangerously They Live* benefited from top talent. Screenwriter Marion Parsonett would later write the noir classic *Gilda* (1944) for Columbia, making Rita Hayworth a major star. Director Robert Florey had helmed the Marx Brothers debut feature *The Coconuts* (1929), but mostly specialized in tight action dramas. He had just finished directing the first Boston Blackie feature at Columbia.

John Garfield was pleased to settle comfortably into a role that connected to his established screen persona, but without having a tough kid backstory. Dr. Lewis is a serious medical professional who studies hard, keeps abreast of all the latest medical topics in his field, and is interested in further advancement. Of course, some of these traits cause him to be duped by Ingersoll, a mentor of his, but that just adds another twist to the narrative.

Nancy Coleman was making her movie debut, having done work in radio. In fact, upon signing with Warner Brothers, she tried to interest the studio in some work her mentor on the airwaves had done. According to an article in the press:

> It isn't often that a young actress gets a chance to "discover" the man who discovered her. But Nancy Coleman who now has the lead opposite John Garfield in *Dangerously They Live* was given the opportunity to show she hasn't forgotten her discoverer. When Nancy was an elevator girl in a San Francisco department store she was trying her level best to break into radio. Then she ran into Sam Dickson, Bay City radio producer, who gave Nancy the chance she'd been waiting for to give up elevators for radio . Now that Nancy is one of the bright hopes around the Warner lot she remembered Dickson and upon looking him up discovered he wasn't working at the moment. Nancy went to see her discoverer and brought back with her three original stories he'd written. Now she's going to act as agent for him— but without the benefit of commission.[41]

Nothing of Dickson's was used, but he did write a play that was performed locally and remained quite successful in radio until his passing in 1974.

Raymond Massey and Moroni Olsen were old veterans and added a great deal to the proceedings, being completely believable as the sinister spies who masqueraded as ordinary successful citizens. Any quirky behavior was dismissed as the idiosyncrasies of a wealthy man. This added layers to the narrative and the consistent series of twists and turns kept it interesting.

Dangerously They Live was released only weeks after Japanese forces attacked Pearl Harbor, and war was declared on America. The war in Europe had escalated into what had become World War 2. Thus, a drama about espionage involving German spies, British intelligence, and a hero-

41 Hollywood with Fredric Othman. *Chico Record.* October 19, 1941

ic American civilian was ready made for period moviegoers. *Film Daily* called the movie:

> Exciting, timely meller dealing with sinister Nazi espionage ring. Good fare for virtually all stands. Robert has directed with eye to pace and suspense and results are good. L. William O'Connell's photography is tip top and so are the performances turned in by the capable cast.[42]

Motion Picture Daily was equally impressed by *Dangerously They Live* stating in their review:

> A new twist to the espionage and counter-espionage story is given Warners' *Dangerously They Live*, an excitingly told and well-done melodrama. The original screenplay by Marion Parsonnet and the direction by Robert Florey maintain suspense throughout to achieve an excellent climax. Miss Coleman, in her largest role to date, delivers exceptionally well.[43]

Again, *Dangerously They Live* is Nancy Coleman's motion picture debut. She would remain active into the television era and live until the year 2000. Years later she would recall that when she and the diminutive Garfield shared a scene in *Dangerously They Live*, he had to stand on a box.

Although considered a B picture and often shown on the bottom half of double-bills, *Dangerously They Live* was a success and the studio was pleased with the outcome. And although he is very good in the role, Garfield didn't find it to be enough of a departure from what he had usually done. He allegedly would confront studio brass with the question, "don't you guys ever make comedies?"

For his next movie, John Garfield was very pleased to finally have the opportunity to appear in a movie for a studio other than Warner Brothers. He was even more pleased to have the opportunity to work at the prestigious Metro-Goldwyn-Mayer (MGM), and to play opposite an actor whom he greatly admired, Spencer Tracy. Warner Brothers was always hesitant about loaning Garfield out for projects that could benefit a rival studio with their popular actor. However, Louis B Mayer wielded enormous power in the film industry, and liked the idea of casting the popular young actor as Danny in their proposed screen version of John Steinbeck's *Torilla Flat*. Garfield was an acquaintance of the author, and asked him to approach MGM with idea of borrowing him from Warners for their movie. While Steinbeck had nothing really to do with the film's

---

42 Dangerously They Live review. *Film Daily*. December 24, 1941.
43 Dangerously They Live review. *Motion Picture Daily*. December 23, 1941

production, he was still respected by Mayer, who was receptive of the idea of hiring Garfield.

Tortilla Flat began production at the end of 1941 and was in production when the Japanese forces bombed Pearl Harbor. John Garfield's response to the war effort would become a significant part of his life for many reasons.

TORTILLA FLAT

Directed by Victor Fleming
Screenplay by John Lee Mahin and Benjamin Glazer based on the book
by John Steinbeck
Produced by Sam Zimbalist
Cinematography by Karl Freund
Edited by James Newcom

Cast:
Spencer Tracy, Hedy Lamarr, John Garfield, Frank Morgan, Akim
Tamiroff, Sheldon Leonard, John Qualen, Donald Meek, Connie Gil-
christ, Allen Jenkins, Henry O'Neill, Mercedes Ruffino, Nina Campena,
Arthur Space, Betty Wells, Harry Burns, Jack Carr, Willie Fung, Charles
Judels, Tim Ryan, Roque Ybarra, Barbara Bedford, Walter Sande, Yvette
Duguay, Larry Wheat, Harry Strang, Guy Rennie, Louis Jean Heydt,
Tito Rnaldo, George Magrill, Bob O'Connor, Emmett Vogan.

Released May 21, 1942
Metro Goldwyn Mayer
105 minutes
Black and White

In perhaps his most unusual film, John Garfield is cast as a working
class Mexican American in a film with no narrative structure. Even John
Steinbeck, author of the original book, wondered how a movie could be
made without being too loosely episodic. But Garfield wanted the role,
enlisted his friend Steinbeck to request him directly to Louis B Mayer, and
Mayer utilized a bit of blackmail to obtain the actor's services, threatening
to reveal Warners not having fulfilled their pledges to some charities.

Garfield plays Danny, a poor but generally happy young man, living in
a California fishing village. His friend Pilon (Spencer Tracy) uses his wit
to obtain any level of bounty, including convincing another friend, Pablo
(Akim Tamiroff) to throw rocks at incoming fisherman, which will cause
them to angrily respond by throwing fish, thus allowing the two some
dinner. Pilon's instinct for manipulation continues when Danny inherits
a couple of houses. His friends all move in with him and it eventually
goes from merrily singing together to conflicts that didn't exist before
the inheritance. Danny is smitten with cannery worker Sweets Ramirez

Spencer Tracy, Hedy LaMarr and John Garfield in Tortilla Flat.

(Hedy LaMarr) while Pilon attempts to steal money from The Pirate (Frank Morgan) until he discovers the man plans to use his funds to buy a candlestick to represent the spirit of a beloved dog who had died. There is further conflict when Danny pawns his guitar to get Sweets a vacuum cleaner. Pilon fears that he and the others will be forced out of the house if she and Danny marry, so he creates a conflict attempting to disrupt their relationship. This causes a fight between him and Pilon, and a fiercer battle at the cannery where Sweets works. Danny is seriously injured and Pilon prays for him. He recovers, marries Sweets, and when his houses burn to the ground, they all realize that it was the inheritance that caused all the conflict. They realize they were happiest when they had nothing.

The most egregious difference between the book and the movie regards the character of Danny, who dies in the original. MGM was noted for insisting upon happy endings, thus the rewrite. The result, however, is indeed episodic as Steinbeck predicted it would be, and while there is a combination of both pleasantness and conflict that blends well and takes the place of a more conventional narrative, *Tortilla Flat* isn't a particularly good film.

Spencer Tracy was likely cast because of his Oscar winning performance as a Portuguese fisherman in *Captains Courageous* (1937), which was also helmed by this film's director, Victor Fleming. However, Tracy would later recall this role quite negatively, according to Bill Davidson's biography, stating: "I never could connect with the fishing village characters John Steinbeck wrote about." MGM executive Eddie Lawrence recalled for Davidson's book that Tracy: "was the kind of alcoholic who could take one drink and be gone. He fell asleep a lot during filming. On *Tortilla Flat*, he was supposed to say a line while he was cutting squid, and he just couldn't manage to get the line right. In the next line, a priest says to him, 'It must have been something you drank, my son.' Tracy broke up so that he couldn't work the rest of the day."[44]

John Garfield got along well with Tracy during filming, despite Tracy's misgivings about the experience, and was pleased to be working with an actor whom he greatly admired. Tracy had a no-nonsense, straightforward approach to his work, and did not understand, nor respect, the method approach Garfield employed, but they still got along fine while working together. Garfield liked the more relaxed, slower pace to filmmaking at MGM, while Tracy disagreed, recalling when he worked at Warner Brothers for *20 Million Years in Sing Sing*, which Garfield remade a few years later. Tracy liked the fast-paced approach to filmmaking that studio utilized.

Garfield also had to tap into both Tracy's and director Fleming's dry, sarcastic sense of humor. When Garfield was shooting his first scene, according to the biography by Larry Swindell:

> The director called a halt and shouted: "For Christ's sake, Garfield, you have to do better than that. I fought like hell to get you in this picture, so don't make me look like a fool." As Tracy snickered in the background, Fleming railed at Garfield some more and they shot the scene again. "Take it easy, Garfield, don't get too good. A lot of your scenes are with Hedy Lamarr. She's not what you'd call unoutclassable, and we can't let that happen. Let's take it again. Be better than you were the first time, but worse than the second."[45]

Garfield eventually realized he was being ribbed and responded with amusement.

In contrast with Spencer Tracy, Hedy Lamarr was quite pleased with her role as Sweets and considered it one of her career-best performances. She had to fight to get the role, and believed that she proved herself handily.

Some critics liked the relaxed approach of *Tortilla Flat* despite not having a discernible plot. They believed the characters were well drawn

---

44 Davidson, Bill. *Spencer Tracy: Tragic Idol*. NY: Dutton. 1988
45 Swindell, Larry. *Body and Soul: The Story of John Garfield*. NY: Morrow. 1975

enough, and performed with such professionalism, that the conflicts made the film entertaining. Bosley Crowther at *The New York Times* stated: "is really a little idyll which turns its back on a workaday world...it is filled with solid humor and compassion—and that is pleasant, even for folks who have to work."[46] However, Kate Cameron, critic for the *New York Daily News* was somewhat less impressed, stating:

> *Tortilla Flat* is the most disappointing picture of the year. The Metro-Goldwyn-Mayer film version of John Steinbeck's book and play, which promised to be another *Grapes of Wrath*, proves to be merely a long-drawn-out picture of California's *Tobacco Road* section. It has to do with the paisanos a people of mixed Spanish and Indian blood, living in the hills above Monterey on the Pacific Coast. They are, according to Steinbeck, a shiftless lot, given to the pursuit of happiness by way of drunkenness, loafing, thievery and lovemaking. Its quick failure on the New York stage might have been an indication to the Metro executives that perhaps the story was not suitable screen material, but nothing daunted, they gave it an elaborate production, assigned three

46 Crowther, Bosley "Review: Tortilla Flat", *The New York Times*, May 22, 1942

of their topnotch players and one borrowed from Warners, and brought in Victor Fleming to direct the story. The grouping of the names of Spencer Tracy, Hedy Lamarr, John Garfield and Frank Morgan is bound to have a potent effect on the box-offices of the country but the fans who go to see their favorites in *Tortilla Flat* will leave the theatre dissatisfied and in a grouchy mood. The paisanos of the picture are not a lovable people and they are not presented with sympathy or affection on the screen. They are a repellent group, led by one Pilon who is completely amoral and a destructionist of the first water. One can find no fault with the performances given by Tracy, Garfield, Morgan, Tamiroff or Miss Lamarr, but the direction is slow and up to the last quarter, when things begin to move a bit, the story is a bore.[47]

Tortilla Flat made a profit for the studio, but was not considered a particularly successful film. It did net an Oscar nomination for Frank Morgan, but reviews didn't make much mention of Garfield's work. Still, John Garfield liked the experience and was satisfied with his performance in this unusual venture.

Tortilla Flat was the only John Garfield film to be released in 1942. During a New York visit, he and his wife visited the Stage Door Canteen, and Garfield got the idea to start the Hollywood Canteen. His attempt to enlist the Hollywood movie community in the project met with especially helpful contributions from Bette Davis, who status in the industry had the clout to get things done. According to the Swindell biography:

> In the very heart of filmland, GIs could gather to hobnob with movie stars who served them refreshments or who would chat and dance with them and sometimes improvise skits. Bette Davis has recalled that most of the stars were getting dolled up for Ciro's one night, and letting their hair down for the Canteen the next.[48]

The Hollywood Canteen attracted top stars like James Cagney, Spencer Tracy, Abbott and Costello, and Gary Cooper, all of whom agreed to appear for free in support of the military.

Despite his liberal progressivism, John Garfield took umbrage at actors like Lew Ayers who were conscientious objectors once America became involved in World War Two. He respected actors like James Stewart and Clark Gable who enlisted to help the war effort. Garfield was taken aback by his 4F ranking when he tried to do the same, and avoided discussing it.

---

47   Cameron, Kate. Tortilla Flat review. *New York Daily News*. May 22, 1942
48   Swindell, Larry. *Body and Soul: The Story of John Garfield*. NY: Morrow. 1975

John Garfield was pleased that his next film was a military drama. The World War Two combat film was becoming its own sub-genre during wartime, and Garfield's next project turned out to be among the best movies of its kind.

AIR FORCE

Directed by Howard Hawks
Screenplay by Dudley Nichols
Produced by Hal Wallis
Cinematography by James Wong Howe
Edited by George Amy

Cast:
John Garfield, John Ridgely, Gig Young, Arthur Kennedy, Charles Drake, Harry Carey, George Tobias, Ward Wood, Ray Montgomery, James Brown, Stanley Ridges, Willard Robertson, Mornoni Olsen, Edward Brophy, Richard Lane, Bill Crago, Faye Emerson, Addison Richards, James Flavin, Murray Alper, Ann Doran, Lynn Baggett, Bill Hunter, Rand Brooks, William Hopper, James Bush, Marjorie Hoshellle, Warren Douglas, Sol Gorss, Bill Edwards, David Horsley, John Estes, Pat Gleason, Charles Flynn, Ruth Ford, James Milican, Bill Hunter, Ross Ford, Frank Marlowe, Bill Kennedy, Allan Lane, Edward and Walter Soo Hoo, Charles Lang, Tom Neal, George Offerman Jr, Harry Lewis, Walter Sande, Dorothy Peterson, Warren Mace, Pat West, Hall Welling, Edwin Stanley, Theodore von Elrtz, Charles Sullivan, Freddie Steele, Maurice Murphy.

Released March 20, 1943
Warner Brothers
124 minutes
Black and White

While the episodic nature of *Tortilla Flat* was often unsettling, the same structure for *Air Force* was somehow effective. More character driven than narrative driven, as much action as exposition, *Air Force* could be considered one of the quintessential World War Two combat films.

The film is set on December 6, 1941 when an air corps bomber named the Mary-Ann was ordered to fly from San Francisco into Hawaii. The film develops the characters who make up the crew, including John Garfield as Sergeant Joe Winocki, a bitter gunner whose bad decision in flight school caused a collision that killed another cadet. When they arrive at their destination it is during the Japanese attack on Pearl Harbor, December 7, 1941. The crew is then ordered to fly to Wake Island, and

John Garfield, George Tobias, and Harry Carey in Air Force.

then the Philippines, both of which are under heavy Japanese attack. The Mary-Ann attacks a fleet of Japanese invaders, but is swarmed and must abort the mission after losing two of its engines. The crew is ordered to bail out, but the pilot, Michael "Irish" Quincannon (John Ridgely) blacks out. Winocki lands the plane safely despite no landing gear, and brings Quincannon to safety. The pilot is told as he's dying that the plane will fly again, even though it is a lost cause. The crew works hard to salvage the bomber, and get it done just as the Japanese army is descending upon the island.

The plot of *Air Force* is a bare bones structure that supports the characters and the battles, which sustain the film. For instance, Harry Carey, appearing in his first film for Warner Brothers since *Kid Galahad* (1937) is the wise old combat veteran who is looking forward to seeing his son that is stationed in the Philippines. When they arrive, he sadly discovers that his son was killed in action before he even got his craft off the ground. *Air Force* is very much an ensemble film, with actors like Garfield, Carey, Ridgley, Arthur Kennedy, Gig Young, and George Tobias. None of the characters are given a great deal of depth, but none are superficial caricatures. There is a genuineness that permeates each role. What helps make *Air Force* more effective in its approach was that all the characters, however different their personalities were and whatever personal matters they were struggling with, were all on the same side and working toward the same goal, which united them

It is Howard Hawks' direction that is especially impressive, especially the overhead shots of soldiers scattering to their battle stations when sirens signal an oncoming Japanese attack. Hawks was a World War One vet, and had an understanding of the material. According to Bruce Orriss' book *When Hollywood Ruled the Skies: The Aviation Film Classics of World War II*, Hawks credited the concept of the film to Henry H. Arnold, who was the army air force Commanding General. It was inspired by his experience on a bomber flight the night before the Pearl Harbor attack. Despite some inaccuracies, the military approved of the script, and production began in May of 1942, with aerial shots and battle sequences filmed first. Dudley Nichols submitted his script in June, and the actors spent a month filming in an accurate mockup of a bomber. Hawks hired William Faulkner to write the scene in which a dying John Ridgley is given affirmation of the Mary-Ann being able to fly again. This caused animosity between Hawks and producer Hal Wallis, who wanted the movie shot as written. Hawks often doesn't get enough credit for his ability to direct action scenes like those in *Air Force*. The special effects are remarkably well done and still hold in the 21st century.

There is some historic realism to *Air Force* in that it depicts a bomber flying to support battles in the Philippines and right into the attack on Pearl Harbor. One of the most striking scenes in the film shows the men listening as President Franklin Roosevelt declares war and they realize they are now officially a part of the battle. The film makes even a modern day viewer feel as if we were watching the war escalate in real time. It felt both realistic and intimate; all of those scenes set solely in the cramped cockpit of the aircraft invite the viewer to get closer to the characters. There admittedly are elements that lean hard into wartime propaganda, and its unfavorable depiction of the Japanese will seem dated as a result. But the viewer becomes so invested in the characters that those elements do not overshadow the rest of the film. *Air Force* may not be, specifically, John Garfield's movie, but he is a stand out in the ensemble cast. The tough cynicism of his character suited his screen persona well.

Jack Warner wanted the film to be released on the one year anniversary of the Pearl Harbor attack, but it took a bit longer to produce, including post-production with its sweeping musical score. When *Air Force* was released in March of 1943, it was a huge hit with moviegoers who wanted powerful films that gave them confidence about the war effort. Often films that relied on the military and action were not as popular with female moviegoers, but *Air Force* was, and ended up becoming the third most popular box office hit of 1943.

The success of *Air Force* was helpful to John Garfield's career, but it wasn't his film. Garfield is eighth-billed in the ensemble cast, even though his scenes are among the film's most powerful, including a more interesting backstory and a heroic landing of a plane after it had been destroyed by enemy fire. Louella Parsons in a June column stated:

> John Garfield has changed his tune since I saw him at Lake Arrowhead a year ago when he was trying to be sent abroad as a foreign correspondent. He intimated then he was through with the movies. But now everything is different. John was very happy over *Tortilla Flat* at MGM. He liked *Dangerously They Live* at Warners and now he has a role Sergeant Joe Winocki in *Air Force* which delights him. The *Air Force* opus by Dudley Nichols deals with the current war and the lads who keep them flying. How- ard Hawks whose *Dawn Patrol* was a hit is directing this timely thriller. A new boy makes his debut, one Bill Crago whom Hal Wallis saw in Washington in February. He was a radio announc- er and Hal impressed with the boy's voice and personality signed him.[49]

Actor Bill Crago, whom Parsons mentions, does appear in *Air Force,* and appears in three other Warner Brothers features released in 1943. And that is when his movie career ended.

A few interesting things happened with John Garfield around the time of *Air Force*. First, his son David was born in July of 1943, joining sister Katherine. Next, Garfield went to court to have his name legally changed from Jules Jacob Garfinkel to John Garfield. And, there was this intrigu- ing press announcement from columnist Harry Mines:

> B. Traven, more skittish than Garbo about meeting folk face to face, continues to hold out against the coaxing tones of Warner officials who would like him to emerge from hiding and meet for a story conference in Mexico City. Traven wrote *Treasure of Sierra Madre* which had John Huston doing a rave to the studio. Letters were exchanged between author and director but nobody ever got together for a handshake. Then Huston went into the navy and that left the fascinating adventure story to Robert Ros- sen, who will tend to the picturization for Jack Warner. Warner yesterday called in Humphrey Bogart, John Garfield and Wal- ter Huston as stars of *Treasure of Sierra Madre*. Their search for the lost silver mines in Mexico provides a strange and exciting psychological study. Meanwhile, Traven manifests, enthusiasm in the entire venture, but by mail only.[50]

---

49 Louella Parsons Column. Hearst Syndicate. June 10, 1942
50 Harry Mines column. *Los Angeles Daily News* February 9, 1943

Of course, *Treasure of Sierra Madre* would not be filmed by Rossen and would not feature John Garfield when it was finally shot and released in 1948, as Garfield left the studio by then. Humphrey Bogart and Walter Huston did appear in the film, with popular B western actor Tim Holt in the role intended for John Garfield. John Huston did direct.

John Garfield continued to be pleased with the films he was doing, as they did not follow a consistently similar pattern as his earlier films had. The actor was especially happy to once again step off the Warner lot and work in a movie for another studio. Arrangements were made to cast Garfield in RKO's production of *The Fallen Sparrow.*

THE FALLEN SPARROW

Directed by Richard Wallace
Screenplay by Warren Duff based on the novel by Dorothy B. Hughes
Produced by Robert Fellows
Cinematography by Nicholas Musuraca
Edited by Robert Wise

Cast:
John Garfield, Maureen O'Hara, Walter Slezak, Patricia Morison, Martha O'Driscoll, Bruce Edwards, John Banner, John Miljan, Hugh Beaumont, Jack Carr, Erford Gage, Andre Charlot, Rosian Galli, William Edmunds, Rita Gould, Cyril Ring, Nestor Paiva, George Lloyd, Sam Goldenberg, Bobby Barber, Mary Halsey, Symona Boniface, Babe Green, Patti Brill, James Conaty, Bud Geary, Sam Harris, Al Rhein, Mike Lally, Lee Phelps, Stella Razeto, Stanley Price, Eric Mayne, Frank O'Connor, Billy Mitchell, Jane Woodworth, Russell Wade, Ed Argesti.

Released August 19, 1943
RKO Radio Pictures
94 minutes
Black and White

The Fallen Sparrow can be considered a transitional film in John Garfield's screen career in terms of his performance and the type of movies in which he'd most often appear. While some of his previous work had flirted with elements of film noir, this was the first one to fully embrace that style. Therefore, *The Fallen Sparrow* is something of a portent to later noir films to come, such as *The Postman Always Rings Twice*, which would define the latter part of his career.

Film noir is a noted movie genre now, but at the time *The Fallen Sparrow* was filmed, the term didn't exist. According to film historian Chris Fujiwara, filmmakers "didn't think of them as 'films noir'; they thought they were making crime films, thrillers, mysteries, and romantic melodramas. The nonexistence of 'noir' as a production category during the supposed heyday of noir obviously problematizes the history of the genre."[51] However, *The Fallen Sparrow* incorporates all of its most basic elements

---

51 Film Noir. Encyclopedia Brittanica (as quoted in....)

with John Garfield playing a brooding character who spends the film searching for answers in regard to his past.

John Garfield plays John "Kit" McKittrick, a Spanish Civil War prisoner who suffered through years of torture. He escaped due to the assistance of lifelong friend Louie Lepitino, a New York police lieutenant. When Louie mysteriously dies, Kit decides to investigate and find out what happened. The police claim Lepitino committed suicide, but Kit doesn't believe them. During his investigation, he comes across disabled refugee Dr. Skaas (Walter Slezak), who is making a study of modern torture methods. Kit finds the doctor's discussion alternately intriguing and unsettling. Kit gets involved with Toni (Maureen O'Hara), who was a witness when Louie fell to his death. Haunted by a past in which he spent years in a dark room where sounds took on extra impact, Kit keeps thinking about the footsteps of a man with a limp that was in charge of his ordeal. As the narrative reveals more, we discover that Kit's unit killed a high ranking official who was close to Adolf Hitler, and Hitler has ordered that the brigade's flag be hung on his wall. Only Kit knows where the flag is. Kit hears a shot and finds his friend Ab (Bruce Edwards), with whom he is staying, dead in the next room, Ab's death is also ruled a suicide, and Kit once again does not believe this conclusion. Kit is confronted by Dr. Skaas, who turns out to be the man with the limp that continues to haunt his mind. Toni, who is connected with the enemy, wants Kit to give up what he knows, but Kit refuses. Toni is given an ultimatum, and chooses to help Kit, but betrays him, claiming her daughter is being held hostage. Kit is drugged but manages to shoot and kill Skaas, and summon police before the drug takes full effect. Kit and Toni arrange to meet in Chicago, but she gets on an airplane headed to Lisbon, causing Kit to realize she remains with the enemy. He arranges her removal from the plane, and takes her place, with the intention to get the flag.

RKO bought the rights to Dorothy Hughes' novel in 1942, but filming was delayed when studio executive William Gordon contacted producer Robert Fellows with the following three concerns:

1. Desire of State Department to maintain friendliest relations with present Spanish government. 2. Possibility of Spain as ally.

3. Offensive to most Latin Americans.

RKO was also contacted by Joseph Breen of the Production Code, stating, "We strongly urge that you consult your Foreign Department as to the advisability of the Spanish angle contained in this picture." Fellows was undaunted and moved forward with the project with no changes.[52]

---

52 Passafiume, Andrea. Fallen Sparrow Review. TCM.com

John Garfield and Maureen O'Hara in the noir drama The Fallen Sparrow.

Several actors were considered for the lead role of Kit, including James Cagney, Cary Grant, Randolph Scott, and George Brent. The role was accepted by John Garfield who realized he could extend beyond his established movie tough guy persona by layering the role with complexities, emphasizing the psychological complexities of the character that were already evident on the printed page. Garfield also lends Kit a touch of vulnerability by playing him as someone who is still traumatized by his past torture and imprisonment. There are times where the characters call his sanity into question, causing the audience to also question whether Kit is really onto something or if certain things are just in his head.

While John Garfield effectively established, and honed, a certain type in his movie career, the character of Kit allowed him to explore other ideas while retaining a decent semblance of his tough guy persona. In certain scenes, Garfield is able to call upon the character he had firmly established in movies, spitting out his dialog like an angry man with a chip on his shoulder. However, this time it is not from a punk who did time in prison and responds with bitterness and rage. Kit is a war hero, he courageously has withheld information under torture, and he is now on a quest to avenge the death of the man who orchestrated his freedom.

Maureen O'Hara had, at this time, established herself in such films as William Dieterle's *Hunchback of Notre Dame* and John Ford's Oscar winner *How Green Was My Valley*. She is decidedly cast against type as an alternately receptive and cunning leading lady whose alliance with the enemy crowds her attraction to Kit. O'Hara would later claim that John Garfield had to stand on a box in their scenes together.

Walter Slezak is very comfortably cast as the disabled villain. The Austrian-born actor made a career out of playing accented bad guys, often in comedies featuring the likes of Abbott and Costello, Bob Hope, and Danny Kaye. He followed up his appearance in *The Fallen Sparrow* with an even more evil character in Alfred Hitchcock's *Lifeboat* (1944).

Director Richard Wallace is not notable as a director of film noir, helming a wide variety of genres in his career, from comedy shorts for Mack Sennett and Hal Roach, to such light fare as *A Girl, A Guy, and a Gob* (1941) and the war drama *Bombardier* (1943). However, when he did direct a noir film, such as *The Fallen Sparrow* or the later *Framed* (1947), he did so with an innate understanding and a keen vision as to how it should be mounted.

Critics were more impressed with the intention of *The Fallen Sparrow* than the execution. *Film Daily* stated:

> For the most part, the film is a confused spy melodrama that has a hard time extricating itself from the maze into which its plot leads. One cannot quibble over the film's suspense, but certainly one can overuse suspense. It is likely that the average fan will be more than a little disappointed to discover that al the fus and all the toying with death are inspired by a Loyalist banner in the possession of Garfield. A further disappointment to the audience will be the nature of the romance between Garfield and Maureen O'Hara, who aids the Nazi ring seeking the banner because she can't help herself. Sympathy is created for her, yet at the end she's in the hands of the FBI.[53]

Audiences responded in a similar way, believing the movie to be too complex to follow despite its being absorbing.

However, in a book about John Garfield, the transitional importance of *The Fallen Sparrow* is evident, as it established the actor as a complex, brooding character the type of which he'd draw upon frequently during post-war cinema.

---

53 Fallen Sparrow Review. Film Daily. August 20, 1943

John Garfield next did a cameo as himself in the Warner Brothers all-star musical comedy *Thank Your Lucky Stars* (1943). It was just a brief bit early in a film that featured vignettes by Humphrey Bogart, Bette Davis, Errol Flynn, Ida Lupino, Olivia de Havilland, and several other stars, while a comic narrative was led by musical comedian Eddie Cantor. After this cameo, it was likely the success of *Air Force* that caused Warner Brothers to next cast John Garfield opposite Cary Grant in the action drama *Destination Tokyo*.

DESTINATION TOKYO

Directed by Delmer Daves
Screenplay by Delmer Daves and Albert Maltz based on a story by Steve Fisher
Produced by Jerry Wald
Cinematography by Bert Glennon
Edited by Christian Nyby

Cast:
Cary Grant, John Garfield, Alan Hale, John Ridgely, Dane Clark, Warner Anderson, William Prince, Robert Hutton, Tom Tully, Faye Emerson, Peter Whitney Warren Douglas, John Forsythe, John Alvin, Bill Kennedy, George Anderson, Warren Ashe, Joy Balrow, William Challee, Benson Fong, Roland Gott, Wing Foo, Bruce Wong, Ya Sing Suing, Eddie Lee, George Lee, James B Leong, Kirby Grant, Whit Bissell, Herbert Gunn, Carlyle Blackwell Jr, John Forrest, Danny Borzage, Cliff Clark, Eddie Hall, Angelo Cruz, William Hudson, William O'Brien, Bill Hunter, Charles Anthony Hughes, Maurice Murphy, Charles Sullivan, Mark Stevens, Dorothy Schoemer, Larry Steers, Duke York, Sailer Vincent, Jay Ward, Wally Walker, John Sylvester, Alan Wilson, Jimmy Evans, Warren Cross, Bob Creasman, Ted Jacques, Cy Malis.

Released December 31, 1943
Warner Brothers
135 minutes
Black and White

As with the previous *Air Force*, John Garfield isn't the star of this wartime action drama, he is part of a supporting ensemble while the lead is effectively played by Cary Grant. It is another strong period drama and, like *Air Force*, a film that John Garfield would continue to consider among his best movies at Warner Brothers.

John Garfield plays Wolf, a womanizing sailor, who along with several others, is assigned to the USS Copperfin submarine run by Captain Cassidy (Cary Grant). Wolf frequently discusses his sexual conquests, thus acquiring the nickname; a penchant of the crew (i.e. the medic (William Prince) is called Pills, et al). Leaving port on Christmas Eve, the Copperfin encounters Japanese aircraft within 24 hours and shoots down

. *John Garfield in* Destination Tokyo.

both planes. One of the enemy soldiers parachutes to safety and when Mike (Tom Tully), a crewmember of the Copperfin, tries to help him out of the water, he is stabbed to death. Tommy, a gunner (Robert Hutton), and Mike's friend, then kills the enemy soldier. Wolf and two other men volunteer to go on a dangerous mission ashore to make important observations for a future attack. Meanwhile, on board the sub, Tommy is suffering from appendicitis and Pills, with no training, must perform necessary surgery with limited resources or the man will die. The subma-

Cary Grant and John Garfield in Destination Tokyo.

rine is then seen by a Japanese destroyer, and its attempts to evade it are unsuccessful. They attack and sink the destroyer, then head back to shore.

Gary Cooper was originally offered the role of Cassidy, but turned it down. Meanwhile, Cary Grant had just turned down the lead in the war drama *Sahara* to be filmed at his home studio Columbia Pictures. Columbia wanted to secure the services of Warner Brothers actor Humphrey Bogart for *Sahara,* so Warner asked that they trade for the services of Cary Grant to star in *Destination Tokyo.*

Delmer Daves had been a successful screenwriter but had never before directed a movie. Cary Grant recalled how Mae West took a chance on casting him in one of her movies when he was starting out, and he liked to do the same for others. Thus, it was he who approved of Daves as the film's director. Daves not only directed this film successfully, he would eventually helm John Garfield again in the film *Pride of the Marines.* Daves co-wrote the screenplay with Albert Maltz, a longtime friend of John Garfield who shared his progressive politics and would later be blacklisted. The director also provided his own son and daughter to play the children of Captain Cassidy.

Patriotic trade ad for Destination Tokyo.

While John Garfield only had a small supporting role in *Destination Tokyo,* his presence is significant to some of the stronger episodes within the narrative framework. However, he wasn't involved in the scene where the soldier must have an emergency appendectomy. This scene is significant because it is based on an actual event which was done on the submarine Sea Dragon in 1942. A 22-year-old pharmacist's mate extracted the appendix of a Seaman using kitchen utensils and other handy items within the limited parameters of his surroundings. This upset the U.S. Surgeon General to the point where the man was nearly court martialed.

However, he was eventually awarded a US Navy Commendation Medal in 2005. There are existing photographs of the operation.

Destination Tokyo is perhaps a bit longer than it needs to be, but it does feel as authentic as it supposedly was (the Navy even reportedly using it for training, arranging screenings for those interested in possibly enlisting). There was a natural quality to many of the conversations between the soldiers, whether they were laced with humor and innuendo (as many of the scenes with Garfield's character were) or heavier ponderings about the war and the families waiting for them back home.

The premiere of *Destination Tokyo* was quite unusual, as reported by John Scott in *The Los Angeles Times*:

> One of the most unusual film reviews in history took place here today. The picture, Warner Brothers' *Destination Tokyo*, was showing in the torpedo room of a submarine, veteran of missions in the South Pacific. A small but highly interested group of newspapermen found the submarine a most impressive locale for the film showing, since *Destination Tokyo* deals with the exciting adventures of an undersea craft of the United States Navy on an unusual mission -- to land a meteorologist on Japanese soil in order to gain data for a bombing raid on Tokyo itself. Following the press preview, the picture was screened for submarine officers and enlisted men and later tonight was unreeled for the general personnel of Mare Island. John Garfield, one of the stars of the production, attended and presented a phonograph to the submariners. Later he visited the Mare Island Hospital, attended a party given for officers' children, and was guest of honor at a dance. Carv Grant and John Garfield as commander and torpedo man, respectively, are well-nigh perfect in their roles. Reaction of the real submarine crew who saw the performances was excellent, which is probably the toughest test of all. Delmer Daves rates special commendation for super direction.[54]

The film's further patriotic promotions included scrap drives as reported in the *Motion Picture Daily*:

> Differing from the usual campaigns of its kind in that no free admissions will be granted, scrap drives under school and civic auspices are being promoted nationally through cooperation of Warners' field staff with local exhibitors in connections with engagements of *Destination Tokyo* starting around the holidays.

---

54 Scott, John. Navy Sees Preview in Submarine. Los Angeles Times. December 23, 1943

Instead of offering free tickets, appeal will be made to the patriotism of students and adults.[55]

Destination Tokyo was an enormous box office success, more than tripling is production costs. When cartoonist Charles Sullivan of the Associated Press started a new syndicated feature entitled Minute Movies, his first five-picture strip telling about a new film story was for *Destination Tokyo*. Meanwhile, exhibitors reported in the trades that *Destination Tokyo* was very well received by their patrons:

> Swell entertainment of the submarine service. Very interesting and educational for some of our boys who are figuring on the Navy. Plenty of action and some comedy.

> Authenticity is what makes this the great picture it is. Excellent performances by Cary Grant and John Garfield. Superb directing and fine photography. Seeing this film is like living the great experience yourself.[56]

Warner Brothers then decided to dust off one of their old properties, Sutton Vane's 1923 play *Outward Bound*, which they had filmed with Leslie Howard under that title in 1930. Hiring screenwriter Daniel Fuchs to give the narrative a wartime setting and some new elements within those parameters, the film was retitled *Between Two Worlds* and it was John Garfield's next movie.

---

55 Warners Aid Scraps. Motion Picture Daily. December 15, 1943
56 What The Picture Did For Me. Motion Picture Herald. June 24, 1944

BETWEEN TWO WORLDS

Directed by Edward A Blatt
Screenplay by Daniel Fuchs from a play by Sutton Vane
Produced by Mark Hellinger
Cinematography by Carl Guthrie
Edited by Rudi Fehr

Cast:
John Garfield, Paul Henreid, Sydney Greenstreet, Eleanor Parker, Edmund Gween, George Tobias, George Coulouis, Faye Emerson, Sara Allgood, Dennis King, Isobel Elsom, Gilbert Emery, Lester Matthews, Patrick O'Moore.

Released May 20, 1944
Warner Brothers
112 minutes
Black and White

This very offbeat fantasy about people caught in a holding period between life and death had been, as indicated in the previous chapter, a hit play in the 1920s and was a 1930 release by Warner Brothers under its original title *Outward Bound*. The Daniel Fuchs screenplay gave it a wartime setting which allowed for the expansion of characters from eight to ten. And while it was a commendable attempt at something different, and has some good scenes, the movie is decidedly not a success.

John Garfield plays a cynical reporter, calling upon the type of character he had established as he made his initial impact on films. He is joined in this limbo by Paul Henreid and Eleanor Parker as a couple who committed suicide, a businessman and his wife (Gilbert Emery and Isobel Elsom), a minister (Dennis King), a sailor (George Tobias), and a housekeeper (Sara Allgood), who carries with her an air of mystery. There is a bartender overseeing the group (Edmund Gwenn) as they await the man who will make the ultimate decision of eternity for each.

The cast is impressive and the acting is good, each performer committed to their role and attempting to make the unbelievable seem believable, which is the key to any successful fantasy. Most of the drama comes from

John Garfield is a cynical reporter between life and death in Between Two Worlds.

their reaction to the realization that they are, indeed, dead, and in limbo, waiting for their fate to be determined. The gamut of emotions is exhibited. The sailor is despondent, realizing he had little chance at life, and that he is leaving behind a loving wife and a new baby. He is angry and upset of having been robbed of a life with them. The others are rebellious, patiently accepting, or nervously attempting to bargain their way out.

Sydney Greenstreet is well cast as the serious, imposing presence who determines the ultimate fate of each. He is unflinching in his decisions, despite the protests with which he is sometimes faced.

While *Between Two Worlds* is an ensemble film, John Garfield does stand out as playing the most interesting character in the group. Rising above the confusion, the rebellion, the protests, and the bargaining, his reporter is not quite aloof in his coldness, but appears to be confronting the situations with the sort of cynical toughness that defined the actor's most notable roles up to this time. While, in retrospect, we realize *The Fallen Sparrow* was a portent to the films he would eventually move into after the war, and which would more effectively define his screen career, John Garfield was still established as a hard talking tough guy when he appeared in *Between Two Worlds*. Under that cynicism we do see just a touch of sentimentality, primarily in his interactions with Sara Allgood's character, who has a significant connection to Garfield's character at the end. We're left with the impression that he will ultimately become a better person in the afterlife thanks to being in her presence.

Unfortunately, this idea was a bit too unconventional for a wartime audience, despite the narrative being updated to be placed in a wartime setting. Wanting uplifting entertainment to take their minds off what was happening overseas, American moviegoers weren't as receptive to a fantasy movie that dwelled on elements of dark introspection, bold cynicism, and end-of-life decisions.

It can be argued that Alfred Hitchcock's *Lifeboat*, released the same year, had a lot of similar elements and was successful and timeless. This is true. However, *Between Two Worlds* was not a realistic story that forced an ensemble to survive by any means necessary. It was about a group of people who had already not survived, and how they responded to a situation over which they no longer had any control. It was an interesting perspective that didn't always work. Sometimes the performances seemed forced and stereotypical, while other times they stumbled into the sort of blatant melodrama that no longer holds up.

Between Two Worlds was the first of only three films Edward Blatt directed and he seems to rely on the narrative and performances to carry the film. It is also the first large part for Eleanor Parker, whose work so impressed John Garfield, he sought her work for a later film, *Pride of the Marines*. Paul Henreid, in his book *Ladies Man: An Autobiography*, recalled director Blatt being "a nice fellow, but inexperienced," and remembered John Garfield as "bright and pleasant, though somewhat naive, and we got along very well. John had to learn card tricks for the

John Garfield, Paul Henried, and Eleanor Parker in Between Two Worlds

part, and he became tremendously excited about them. He practiced constantly, and bored all of us with them."[57]

Bosley Crowther in *The New York Times* was unimpressed with *Between Two Worlds*, echoing the sentiments of most critics, stating in his review:

> Probably because they figured that these are troubled times in which people are more than commonly interested in their spiritual destinies, Warner Brothers have shaken the dust from Sutton Vane's old *Outward Bound* and have remade it in a modern version under the title *Between Two Worlds*. Obviously the Warners were tempting fate themselves, for this study of death and the hereafter is notoriously wistful and grim. It has very little to offer in the popular comedy line. And it is curiously depressing in its exposure of human faults. But it is also fascinating in its fanciful treatment of death, and response to its spiritual enchantment may be expected from this picture. In modernizing the story, which was first presented as a play in 1923—and then, as a motion picture, in 1930, with Leslie Howard—the Warners have started activities in the London of the present day and have

---

57   Henreid, Paul and Julius Fast. *Ladies Man: An Autobiography.* NY: St Martin's Press, 1984

shipped a cargo of passengers, most of whom were killed in a bombing raid. The two passengers, originally known as the "half ways," are here presented as a young pianist and his wife, he a shell-shocked Free Frenchman and she an English girl. And to the passenger list is added an American merchant seaman, who is ultimately reconciled to dying by the knowledge that he died for a cause. Otherwise the story, in substance, is precisely the same as it was in the original. It is the story of these several passing souls who find themselves sailing on a strange ship to a mysterious beyond. Each of them has some phobia or frustration which is gnawing at his heart (if heart you can call it in a dead man). And the resolution or resignation of their personal ills are finally accomplished by the Examiner, who comes aboard at the journey's end. In treatment, the present production aims plainly to plant the fact in the very beginning that the passengers aboard this ship are all dead. Thus, the eerie realization, which came later and slowly in the play, is lost completely in the picture, with its consequent stunning effect. Otherwise this production is competent, though the script runs entirely to discourse, and Director Edward A. Blatt has managed to move his people around with some pain. The performances are generally satisfactory.[58]

There is definitely some interesting world-building in this film regarding the afterlife: the fact that the characters are physically sailing there, and have that time to come to term with their fates. The fact that Henreid and Parker's characters committed suicide and therefore get a different fate from the others was also an interesting twist. But despite some heartbreaking moments involving a couple of the characters realizing they are dead, the film really doesn't come to life until Sydney Greenstreet shows up. It is fascinating to hear the fates handed out to each character based on who they are as a person and their deeds in life. But the ending is a bit of a cop-out for two of the characters. Some critics opined that the first part of the film might have been more intriguing if we didn't know that the characters were dead until later in the movie.

While appearing in this movie, John Garfield was also going to another soundstage on the Warner lot for the all-star feature *Hollywood Canteen*, based on the project he and Bette Davis put together for servicemen. He and Davis discussed the history of the club they founded, and servicemen are seen enjoying the talents of Jack Benny, The Andrews Sisters, Eddie Cantor, Joe E. Brown, even Roy Rogers and Trigger. *Hollywood Canteen*, which was released as a film later in 1944, was notable for being the

---

58 Crowther, Bosley. Between Two Worlds review. The New York Times. May 6, 1944

first appearance of Joan Crawford, after having bought out her MGM contract over a year earlier. Tired of what she considered to be lackluster roles, Crawford spent a lot of her own money to get out of her contract, and her first starring role at Warners, in *Mildred Pierce*, netted her an Oscar.

PRIDE OF THE MARINES

Directed by Delmer Daves.
Screenplay by Albert Maltz from a book by Roger Butterfield, adapted by Marvin Browsky
Produced by Jerry Wald
Cinematography by J. Peverell Marley
Edited by Owen Marks

Cast:
John Garfield, Eleanor Parker, Dane Clark, John Ridgely, Rosemary DeCamp, Ann Todd, Tom D'Andrea, Ann Doran, Warren Douglas, Don McGuire, Rory Mallinson, Mark Stevens, Anthony Caruso, Moroni Olsen, Leonard Bremen, William Hudson, Dick Rich, Harry Shannon, Dave Willock, Bud Wolfe, Michael Browne, John Compton, Frank Faylen, Mary Gordon, William Haade, James Conaty, George Reed, Charles Evans, John Miles, William Hudson, Fred Kelsey, John Sheridan, Charles Sherlock

Released August 24, 1945.
Warner Brothers
Running time: 120 minutes
Black and White

Pride of the Marines is a powerful drama based on a true story about Al Schmid, an honest, self-aware, hardworking man who avoids relationships and balks at marriage, but meets a girl with whom he connects well. However, the bombing of Pearl Harbor inspires Al to enlist. He is blinded in battle and tries to rehabilitate and learn to live with his affliction with the help of his girlfriend upon his being discharged. The film went through several title changes during preparation and production, including *This Love of Ours* and *Al Schmid: Marine* before finally settling on the title that was used.

According to a June, 1944 column by Hedda Hopper, the film was almost postponed indefinitely:

> John Garfield won't do *Al Schmid, Marine*. That picture and all war pictures are postponed indefinitely at Warners. Garfield goes

Ad for Pride of the Marines.

to Metro on loan-out for Hedy Lamarr, but says he. "I wish I'd been loaned out TO Hedy Lamarr instead."[59]

Of course these plans changed, and no film with John Garfield playing opposite Hedy Lamarr was ever made, although they had worked together in *Tortilla Flat*.

Perhaps the idea that the film about Al Schmid was not so much a war picture but a domestic drama is what caused the studio to change its mind. By October, 1944, Edwin Schallert announced a director had been chosen:

> Progress of Delmer Daves in managing the war-linked story as director apparently intrigues Warner Bros, nabobs because he has now been chosen to guide *This Love of Ours*, which is about Sgt. Al Schmid. This will be more of a home front than a war area narrative, dealing with the loyal love of the heroine, as well as the experiences of Schmid. John Garfield is the male star. Daves began his directing with *Destination Tokyo*, after career as a writer.[60]

Every aspect of this film works perfectly. The characters are developed in a manner that is alternately amusing and compelling. John Garfield, as Al Schmid, is cocky and assured, but still likeable. His initially tumultuous date with Ruth (Eleanor Parker) develops into a romance that eschews schlock for snappy dialog, a penchant for wartime movies, especially at Warner Brothers. Their relationship's development is at a perfect spot when the film shifts to Al's enlistment. He proposes to Ruth on the station platform.

Following the true events of Al Schimd's life, the military scenes take place at the Battle of the Tenaru River on the Pacific island of Guadalcanal on August 21, 1942. Most of the marines are killed in the battle, but Schmid's crew manages to kill over 200 enemy soldiers. Schmid is blinded by a grenade blast. These scenes are a shift in action from the first third of the film, director Delmer Daves using quick edits and an effective succession of shots to convey the horror of battle and the triumph of the marines. The quiet scenes, bathed in darkness and making use of closeups, are especially effective. When Al is left alone to battle, Garfield's running dialog with himself adds an even greater intensity to the battle scene.

The final third is the most dramatically intense, with Schmid having to adjust to civilian life as a blind man. He resents relying on others, and while he is angered by his disability, he doesn't know how to confront and overcome it. An operation attempting to restore his sight fails. He

---

59   Hedda Hopper column. *Los Angeles Times*. June 7, 1944
60   Daves Will Direct Story of Al Schmid. *Los Angeles Times*. October 5, 1944

John Garfield and Eleanor Parker in Pride of the Marines.

doesn't believe he is worthy of Ruth's love, but with the help of his war buddy Lee Diamond (Dane Clark) she is able to convince him of her devotion.

Eleanor Parker is charming, amusing, and compelling in a challenging role where she must not only be striking and appealing, but emotionally affected and strong. Her character has to adapt to her husband's handicap, but also work through his insecurities about being worthy of her. It is a challenging role, and she rises to the occasion, offering one of her finest performances.

There is a scene in the military rehabilitation center where several veterans discuss going home and dealing with their various disabilities. One man says, "I'll probably go back and find that some Mexican has taken my job!" The camera reveals that, among the vets, is a disabled Latino soldier. The man apologizes, stating, "you're Mexican, but you're different." "No," the Latino man states, "I'm just like all the other Mexicans who fought." It is a very pointed scene, and while brief and not an organic part of the central narrative, it resonates even after the movie has concluded. Screenwriter Albert Maltz added this to his screenplay to make a statement.

Pride of the Marines was an enormous hit for Warner Brothers both critically and commercially. Bosley Crowther of *The New York Times* called the film "a splendid documentation of a dramatic crisis in a hero's life," with performances that were "all unqualifiedly excellent. To say that this picture is entertaining to a truly surprising degree is an inadequate recommendation. It is inspiring and eloquent of a quality of human courage that millions must try to generate today."[61] *Variety* called it "a two-hour celluloid saga which should inspire much pride for many. As an entertainment film with a forceful theme, so punchy that its 'message' aspects are negligible, it is a credit to all concerned."[62]

The film was fairly expensive for the time, but its box office receipts tripled its production costs. Most of this is due to the often clever and elaborate promotional ideas employed by some theaters. In the August 11, 1945 issue of *Motion Picture Herald* an article stated:

> A full day of varied activities marked the world premiere of Warners' *Pride of the Marines*, held Tuesday in Philadelphia. A group of approximately 25 Marines were welcomed at the Mayor's office at the start of the day. At that time, several of the men where awarded decorations in the Mayor's reception room at City Hall. Al Scmid, Marine veteran who was blinded on Guadalcanal and hwho is the hero of the picture, was the official host. In the afternoon, a group of 50 First Division Marines participated in. an outdoor celebration with the Northeast Chamber of Commerce and the American Legion Post of Frankford. Following this, a cocktail reception was held preceeding the banquet at the Bellevue-Stratford Hotel. The public premiere of *Pride of the Marines* took place at the Mastbaum theater in Philadelphia.

Pride of the Marines holds up as one of the best wartime dramas in American cinema, as well as one of John Garfield's career-great performances. Garfield nails his character's cocky attitude in the first half of the film, and heartbreakingly portrays him coming to terms with his blindness in the second act. It's devastating to watch him after the surgery to attempt to fix his eyesight fails, as he's begging the doctor to bring

---

61 Pride of the Marines review. *New York Times.* August 25, 1945
62 Pride of the Marines review. *Variety* August 31, 1945

a flashlight closer to his eyes, anything to believe that his eyesight isn't totally gone. A scene where he goes home for Christmas and confronts his family and Ruth for the first time after he returns home is very emotional as he struggles to keep it together.

This would continue to be one of John Garfield's favorite projects, mostly because he was so impressed with the man he portrayed. According to Louella Parsons in her column:

> John Garfield says the really wonderful thing about Al Schmid, the blind marine, is his philosophy about his affliction. He never acts or talks as if he were sightless. Johnny's picture, is based on Schmid's life and experiences. When Garfield was in Philadelphia making the film, he promised Al he would bring back the first print as soon as it completed. "Yes," said Schmid, "I want to be the first to see it." It will be shown to him and his in a projection room with Mrs. Schmid explaining to her husband as the movie unfolds.

The real Al Schmid became a celebrity as much for this movie as for his wartime heroism and sacrifice, and was awarded the Navy Cross. Schmid only lived to be 62 years old, his wife Ruth surviving him by 20 years. Both are buried at Arlington National Cemetery.

THE POSTMAN ALWAYS RINGS TWICE

Directed by Tay Garnett.
Screenplay by Harry Ruskin and Niven Busch based on the novel by
James M. Cain
Produced by Carey Wilson
Cinematography by Sidney Wagner
Edited by George White

Cast:
John Garfield, Lana Turner, Cecil Kellaway, Hume Cronyn, Leon Ames,
Audrey Totter, Alan Reed, Jeff York, A. Cameron Grant, Joel Friedkin,
Wally Cassell, Morris Ankrum, Edward Earle, Jim Farley, Tom Dil-
lon, Phillip Ahlm, Harold Miller, Reginald Simpson, John Albam, Dick
Crockett, James Darrell, Jeffrey Sayre, Walter Ridge, Charles Williams
John Sullivan, Dorothy Phillips, Howard Mitchell, Don Anderson, Rob-
ert Haines, King Baggott, Byron Foulger, Betty Blythe, Jim Farley, Paul
Bradley, Jack Chefe, Paul Kruger, Virginia L. Randolph, Garry Owen,
Helen McLeod, Sandra Morgan, Dan Quigg, Hilda Rhodes George
Noisom, Brick Sullivan.

Released May 2, 1946.
MGM
Running time: 113 minutes
Black and White

The Postman Always Rings Twice features another one of John Garfield's
career-best performances. He plays a well-drawn character with substance that allows him to use elements of the screen persona that he had
perfected, as well as dig deeper emotionally. Lana Turner forever considered it her best work. Tay Garnett's direction was one of the other reasons
for the movie's success. And it is based on a book that was considered
impossible to film.

James M. Cain's novel was released in 1934 and at the time, Meriam
C. Cooper of RKO studios sent a synopsis to the Breen office to see
if a screen version was possible. The censors found it too objectionable

Tay Garnett directs John Garfield and Lana Turner in The Postman Always Rings Twice.

for cinema at a time when the Production Code was just beginning to be enforced. The project was then shelved. Both Warner Brothers and Columbia Pictures also considered it, but came to the same conclusion. It was MGM that finally went ahead and filmed the challenging material, which is curious in that this was a studio that preferred wholesome fare. Even when the film was completed and a box office success, Louis B. Mayer professed to have hated it.

According to press releases, Lana Turner was chosen quickly for the female lead but John Hodiak was considered for the male. But when Hodiak and Turner didn't ignite much interest in their previous film, *Marriage is a Private Affair* (1944) he was dropped from the project. The *Los Angeles Times* reported:

> *The Postman Always Rings Twice,* James Cain's sensational novel of a decade ago, has been put on the schedule at MGM. The story was bought by the studio at the height of its success, but because of its subject matter, It was frowned upon by the Hays office. However, since two other Cain works, *Double Indemnity* and the currently shooting *Mildred Pierce,* have proved that the authors realistic style can be tamed down sufficiently for cinematic adaptation, interest

John Garfield and Lana Turner embody pragmatic cynicism in The Postman Always Rings Twice.

in *Postman* was revived. Niven Busch will do the screenplay and Carey Wilson will produce. Lana Turner and Gregory Peck have been mentioned for the leads.[63]

Of course, Gregory Peck did not end up taking the lead, but would work with John Garfield in a future classic.

Apparently, Lana Turner wanted to work opposite John Garfield, so MGM arranged to borrow him from Warner Brothers for the project. Garfield was drawn to the material because he recognized the strong writing, and was impressed that Cain's sordid novel was able to be filmed at all.

John Garfield plays Frank Chambers, a drifter who hitches a ride with a man who turns out to be a district attorney, Kyle Sackett (Leon Ames). Frank ends up at a diner, getting a job with an older affable man named Nick Smith (Cecil Kellaway) and his wife Cora (Lana Turner). While Nick is older and quite ordinary looking, Cora is younger and strikingly beautiful. The ruggedly handsome Frank is attracted to Cora and they develop an affair. Falling for each other, they plan to murder Nick and take over his diner business together. After a botched attempt where Nick recovers not realizing their intention, the restless Frank believes there is no future in this situation and takes off for Los Angeles. He runs into Nick again, who talks him into returning, with the promise

63   Hanna, David. Film News I Review. *Los Angeles Times.* January 5, 1945.

of something big happening. Frank returns and finds Cora to be rather distant, while Nick happily announces he is moving to Canada to look after an ailing sister (along with Cora) and selling the diner. Cora lapses into desperation and Frank finds her late at night planning to stab herself, so he once again agrees to kill Nick. He and Cora try to set up a road accident with Nick, where it looks like he perishes in a crash while driving drunk. In front of Sackett, who happens to come to the diner to use their gas pump, Cora and Frank stage an argument where it is revealed Frank and Nick are drunk. Sackett follows their car which plummets over a cliff after Frank hits Nick in the head, but Frank gets caught in the car and is injured while Nick is killed. Sackett arrives on the scene and blames Cora. Cora's lawyer, Arthur Keats (Hume Cronyn) gets a written confession from Cora but keeps it in a safe while having his client arrange a plea bargain for manslaughter, only getting probation. Cora and Frank marry to avoid testifying against each other, and publicity about the incident results in the diner becoming a popular attraction and very lucrative. Keats' assistant Kennedy (Alan Reed) has a falling out with him, retrieves Cora confession from his safe, and tries to use it to blackmail her and Frank. Frank beats him into giving up the confession paper and destroys it. Cora then confronts Frank and tells him that she realizes while she was away caring for her ailing mother he had an affair with another woman (Audrey Totter). She then reveals she is pregnant and they decide the life they bring into the world will make up for the one they destroyed. After a day at the beach, Cora is killed when Frank gets in a crash on the way home. Frank is about to be charged with murdering her, even though it was an accident, but Sackett reveals he has evidence that Frank killed Nick. Frank realizes that while he is innocent of killing Cora, he did kill Nick, and his execution will be for that crime.

As stated in the chapter on *The Fallen Sparrow*, John Garfield's career began moving into film noir, especially during the post-war period when that style of filmmaking was enjoying what is now considered its classic period. *The Postman Always Rings Twice* is a quintessential example of noir. With a shimmering Lana Turner as a classic femme fatale, Garfield as a drifter who is easily led astray, the doomed love and murderous exploits of these central characters, the developing film noir style was clear within this film's structural foundation. The characters in *Postman* reflect the attitude of adults who lived through the Depression and a World War while a feeling of disillusioned pessimism overtook their base romanticism. Turner and Garfield exhibit this psyche, working very comfortably within the dark imagery and hushed tones, while Tay Garnett's direction keeps the film compelling and suspenseful.

Hume Cronyn scores as a wily defense lawyer with John Garfield and Lana Turner in The Postman Always Rings Twice.

Edwin Schallert of *The Los Angeles Times* was suitably impressed with the film, stating in his review:

> Payment for a crime may not be direct but it is inevitable. That much for the moralists, *The Postman Always Rings Twice* proffers as a culminating touch. The stars of the film are Lana Turner and John Garfield, though noteworthy performances are given by Hume Cronyn, who almost steals the show for a while; Cecil Kellaway and Leon Ames. Alan Reed has some dire scenes to play as a blackmailer. Audrey Totter contributes an alluring note in one episode. Altogether cast, adapters Harry Ruskin and Niven Busch, Director Tay Garnett and Producer Carey Wilson have done quite a job with the James M. Cain novel.[64]

It is of some significance that Schallert makes reference to two other noir features, Alfred Hitchcock's *Rebecca* (1940) and Fritz Lang's *Scarlet Street* (1945). It shows how the style was emerging as early as the pre-war era, gradually developing and fully establishing itself in post-war American cinema. Of course the term film noir did not exist. That

---

64 Schallert, Edwin. Postman Always Rings Twice review. *Los Angeles Times*. May 8, 1946

John Garfield plays a man whose passions are his undoing in The Postman
Always Rings Twice.

became popularized by the book *Panorama du film noir americain* (1955)
by Raymond Borde and Étienne Chaumeton.

Author James Cain believed Lana Turner was perfectly cast as Cora
and was suitably impressed with her performance. Garfield and Turner
have really great chemistry in this movie and that's a big reason why it
is such a success. The scene at the beginning in which their characters
are first introduced is one of the best in the movie—Cora's lipstick rolls
across the floor, we get a close up of Frank's reaction, and then we see
what he sees as the camera reveals Cora, panning up from her feet. They
both come off as tough but vulnerable, and one gets the sense that they
really do care for each other, despite everything, which makes the ending
that much more tragic, especially for Garfield. This role feels like a big
step in the evolution of his screen persona.

Sadly, around the time this movie was being filmed, John Garfield suffered a terrible personal tragedy. In March of 1945, Garfield's daughter
Katherine had a sudden allergic reaction and died. She was only 7 years
old. Method actor Garfield took the pain of this heartbreaking situation
and used it to strengthen his performance. It was a sort of therapy helping him emotionally survive a tragic loss from which he could never fully
recover. Another daughter, Julie, was born the following January.

The Postman Always Rings Twice was popular with moviegoers, many of whom were attracted to the lurid material, which is the very reason Louis B. Mayer disliked it. Exhibitors found novel ways to promote the film, including a theater owner in Buffalo, NY:

> An extensive campaign featured by tie-ins with the book was arranged for the playdate of *The Postman Always Rings Twice* at the Buffalo theater, New York. The campaign was the work of Charles B Taylor, advertising director for Shea's Buffalo theaters. Book tie-ups were arranged with the Grant department store, the Ford drug store circuit, the Ulbrick stores and the Queen City bookstore. The Grant display featured a 40 x 60 blow-up of Lana Turner and John Garfield, 8 x 10 stills, posters tying in the picture and the book, and a revolving platform stacked with books.[65]

Earning four times its production costs, *The Postman Always Rings Twice* would remain among the best work of either lead actor

John Garfield was becoming as restless as the drifter he played in this movie. Now wanting to explore other possibilities in the post-war era of cinema, Garfield felt his Warner Brothers work wasn't offering as many possibilities. He was looking into independent production, realizing that at the end of 1946, his contract with Warners would be concluding. That was still some months away, though, so he started work on his next film at the studio.

---

65 Book Angle Stessed for Campaign on 'Postman' *Motion Picture Herald.* July 27, 1946

NOBODY LIVES FOREVER

Directed by Jean Negulesco
Screenplay by W.R. Burnett
Produced by Robert Buckner
Cinematography by Arthur Edeson
Edited by Rudi Fehr

Cast:
John Garfield, Geraldine Fitzgerald, Walter Brennan, George Tobias, George Colouris, Faye Emerson, Robert Shayne, Richard Gaines, Dick Erdman, James Flavin, Ralph Peters, Marion Martin, Ralph Dunn, George Meader, William Forrest, Grady Sutton, Allan Ray, Harry Seymour, Roger Neury, Jack Wise, Robert Arthur, Alex Havier, John Barton, Ted Billings, Jack Gordon, Jack Chefe, Kit Guard, John Conte, Adrian Droseshout, Herschel Graham, Joel Friedkin, William Edmunds, William H. O'Brien, Virginia Patton, Albert Van Antwerp, Monty O'Grady, Lee Phelps, Paul Power, Edward Rickard, Cyril Ring, Wallace Scott.

Released November, 11 1946.
Warner Brothers
Running time: 100 minutes
Black and White

With a script by W.R Burnett, whose forte was rugged action dramas, *Nobody Lives Forever* appeared like it was going to be another aggressive actioner that would be more akin to the type of John Garfield used to do, and less like the noir he was beginning to explore. While that is true to an extent, *Nobody Lives Forever* is presented by director Jean Negulesco in the same manner as noir, with some discernibly similar elements.

The sort of gangster films that Burnett was known for writing had been a bit out of vogue in cinema during the war. They were more popular during the Depression era. However, the success of the low budget Monogram studio's film *Dillinger* (1945) caused studios to realize that gangster

A pensive John Garfield in Nobody Lives Forever.

pictures were in again. Combining the elements of a classic crime action-er with some of the stylistic methods of film noir made *Nobody Lives Forever* more interesting than its rather standard production would indicate.

Director Negulesco had experience as an artist and his sharp visual sense helped make his first feature-length directorial effort, *The Mask of Dimitrios* (1944) a big hit, despite it featuring two character actors – Peter Lorre and Sydney Greenstreet – as leads. This led to other, similar assignments, finally resulting in *Nobody Lives Forever*.

John Garfield plays Nick Blake, a soldier who has been honorably discharged from the service due to an injury. Returning to New York, Nick is met by his old pal Al (George Tobias), and looks forward to reconnecting with his girl Toni (Faye Emerson). Nick had left $50,000 with Toni and is pleased when told that she now runs a nightclub. When he meets up with Toni, he discovers that she is now connected with Chet King (Robert Shayne) and no longer has his money. Nick has to strong-arm the cash out of King, and kisses, then slaps, Toni goodbye. He then heads to Los Angeles with Al to reconnect with an old con man from his past named Pop Gruber (Walter Brennan). Pop is too old for the

John Garfield courts Geraldine Fitzgerald in Nobody Lives Forever.

rackets, so Nick connects with con man Doc Ganson (George Colouris), through Pop, despite some past conflicts. Nick, a ladies man, plans to swindle money out of Gladys, a wealthy widow (Geraldine Fitzgerald), but he ends up falling in love with her. When Gladys finds out the truth about Nick, he admits it and plans to leave, but she has fallen in love and doesn't care about his past. Toni arrives, and gets involved with Doc, who then kidnaps Gladys. Pop, Nick, and Al go after them, and while Gladys is rescued, both Doc and Pop are killed.

Nobody Lives Forever has been dismissed as forgettable due to its following a film as strong and impactful as *The Postman Always Rings Twice*. In fact, when taken in the context of John Garfield's filmography up to this point, it fits rather neatly in his career's progression. It is another role that, while not complex on the surface, does allow the actor to exhibit the tough guy qualities he had established early, and also the dark and brooding elements he has since added to his screen persona.

Coming out of his experiences as a solider at war, the Nick character does not take anything for granted. He is pleased and delighted to see New York City outside his window. He is delighted by being greeted by old friend Al. And he eagerly heads out to see his girl Toni who had been holding onto his $50,000, especially after being informed by Al that she runs a nightclub. Even when they get to his old apartment, now inhabited by an absent Toni, and the place is in disarray, Nick maintains his enthusiasm. It is not until a pipe is found on the bureau that his pragmatism kicks in. Nick is from the rackets, he understands underhandedness immediately upon noticing it.

It is this immediate and jarring experience that causes Nick to relapse into the tough character that had been suppressed by his serious responsibilities as a solider on the battlefield. He confronts Chet King alone in his office, and says, "I don't want to get tough unless I have to." He leaves with his money, kissing Toni goodbye, and slapping her for good measure as he leaves.

These opening scenes establish a lot of important details. We get to know Nick's backstory, and understand his place in the film's narrative. We don't hear much more about his stint in the army. It appears that experience has not had lasting impact. Nick very quickly reverts back to who he once was during the war.

The only thing that tangentially connects us to Nick and the military is the time away. Returning soldiers had to adapt to the shifting culture of the post war era, having left as the Depression had slowly concluded. Nick has to respond to the changes in crime and criminality in this same era. The result is his mixing with men who had once been petty thieves, far beneath his lofty level before the war. The once ambitious Doc is jealous of how far Nick had gone, and that he could now settle back into any kind of leadership position upon his return.

These aspects of the narrative are quintessential W.R. Burnett, examining crime and criminals and their response to their surroundings. Burnett's protagonists (Rico Bandello, et al) always find a way to achieve within the culture's parameters. However, unlike his other characters, Nick's rise is not meteoric. He does not fall from grace and die in the end.

The film noir elements that add another layer to Burnett's screenplay are mostly visual. Director Negulesco keeps things dark and confined for the most part, even though Nick is operating in big cities like New York and Los Angeles. The visuals are dark, Nick is presented as quiet and smoldering when he is not being more typically aggressive and demanding. Garfield's quieter, lighter scenes opposite Geraldine Fitzgerald as Gladys show another aspect of Nick's personality, but he is forthcoming with her, admitting, "guys like me never change."

Unlike a typical noir, there is no femme fatale in the classic sense. Toni effectively represents the conniving woman with the power to distract men and who wields some sensual powers over them with her presence.

George Tobias, Walter Brennan, and John Garfield hatch a scheme in Nobody Lives Forever.

When she comes to Los Angeles and tricks her way into the proceedings, it is with little effort borne from vast experience.

The acting in *Nobody Lives Forever* is exceptional. George Tobias, who worked frequently with John Garfield, plays the classic supportive friend who is willing to do what is necessary to support the central character. He exhibits a canny loyalty and is not the sort of bumbling presence Ralph Peters is called upon to play as Doc's henchman. Faye Emerson is sleek and alluring, Geraldine Fitzgerald earnest and believing, Walter Brennan savvy and experienced, George Colouris dark and evil, Robert Shayne slimy and untrustworthy. They all settle into these general screen stereotypes and give them a depth and substance that extends beyond their parameters.

Thus, *Nobody Lives Forever*, while not the artistic triumph that *The Postman Always Rings Twice* had been, was not a simple programmer. It offers much more and is an interesting example of how the type of movie John Garfield used to appear in so frequently was now augmented for a different style and approach to filmmaking. It says as much about the historical content of post-war cinema as it does about the trajectory of John Garfield's career.

Of course, these terms and methods were not of notice as the films were being made, only understood in retrospect as we study film's historical

John Garfield in a wardrobe shot in preparation for Nobody Lives Forever.

progression. So critics only responded to the basic aesthetics, like this review from the *San Francisco Examiner:*

> The title of *Nobody Lives Forever*, current John Garfield starrer, could have been shortened to *Nobody Lives. Period.* That's about the way things turn out in this latest gangster film. By the time the finale rolls around, giving you a chance to exhale, several snide individuals have been violently liquidated and it served them right. But mob world murders, sluggings, kidnaping and other nefarious human endeavors do not monopolize the plot. There's more than a fleeting romance understanding handled by Geraldine Fitzgerald and Garfield. The best angle is Garfield's honest portrayal of an ex-soldier who would forget his gangster past and try to rebuild his life on a new found philosophy born of battlefield experiences. While *Nobody Lives Forever* presents few surprises following the pattern of most underworld dramas, forthright acting by the cast and the polished direction of Jean

Negulesco, build up a film story with unabating suspense and action.[66]

Both John Garfield and Geraldine Fitzgerald were wrapping up their tenure at Warner Brothers, neither having signed the extended contract they were offered. Garfield's last film for his long time studio would star him in a serious drama opposite Joan Crawford, who was new to the studio after a long tenure with MGM. She had just scored triumphantly in her Warner debut, *Mildred Pierce*, and requested Garfield for her leading man in *Humoresque*.

---

66   Nobody Lives Forever review. *San Francisco Examiner* October 9, 1946

HUMORESQUE

Directed by Jean Negulesco
Screenplay by Clifford Odets and Zachary Gold from the short story by
Fannie Hurst
Produced by Jerry Wald
Cinematography by Ernest Haller
Edited by Rudi Fehr

Cast:
John Garfield, Joan Crawford, Oscar Levant, J. Carrol Naish, Joan Chandler, Tom D'Andrea, Peggy Knudsen, Ruth Nelson, Craig Stevens, Paul Cavanagh, Richard Gaines, John Abbott, Robert Blake, Tommy Cook, Don McGuire, Fritz Leiber, Peg La Centra, Nestor Paiva, Harlan Briggs, Patricia Barry, An Lawrence, Angela Greene, Esther Michelson, Richard Walsh, Leo Wonder, Sylvai Arsian, Eric DeLamarter, Creighton Hale, Paul Panzer, Edwina Pierse, Louis Quince, Ramon Ros, Gary Armstrong, Janet Barrett, Monte Blue, Gino Corrado, James Carlisle,, Bess Flowers, John J. Darby, Marion Gray, Leota Lorraine, Oliver Cross, Kenneth Gibson, Jack Deery, Oliver Cross, Kenneth Gibson, Ethelreda Leopold, Florence Wix, Max Linder, Fred Rapport, King Lockwood, Foster Phinney, Monty O'Grady, Harold Miller, Don Turner.

Released January 25, 1947
Warner Brothers
Running time: 125 minutes
Black and White

Closing out his contract with Warner Brothers, John Garfield returned to the studio after completing work on *The Postman Always Rings Twice* and found himself cast opposite Joan Crawford in *Humoresque*. Realizing she would be the star of the film, and would command top billing, he turned the project down, accepting suspension and even allowing the press to announce that he and the studio parted ways. According to the press:

> John Garfield and Warner Bros, have called it quits, according to the actor. This was in the air, of course, although Garfield had a contract which was to run until February. There was very little prospect of anything but the player's taking another

suspension, and he had had several protracted ones during his association, because he wasn't satisfied with stories. Last night a spokesman for Jack Warner denied that Garfield's pact has ended at all. "We haven't called it quits and we haven't taken. *Humoresque* (announced previously for the star) off the schedule," he said. Garfield's latest picture for Warners was the very successful *Pride of the Marines* and on loan to Metro he has since acted in *The Postman Always Rings Twice*, which is still to be released. He has his independent plans that will likely include one film a year for M.G.M., and may also sign with R.K.O.[67]

John Garfield changed his mind because his wife was pregnant with their third child, and he realized his suspension would prevent him from securing work elsewhere for a time. He accepted the project and did his best with it.

Joan Crawford had been a major star at MGM, but her last several films were not successful. Upon leaving that studio and signing with Warner Brothers, Joan's first film with Warners (other than a cameo in *Hollywood Canteen*) was *Mildred Pierce* which not only netted her an Oscar, it was so enormously successful, the film accounted for half of the studio's box office for the year 1945. Joan Crawford was hot again, so she got top billing despite playing clearly a supporting part while Garfield's character is central to the narrative. Joan told Louella Parsons:

> I have been criticized for accepting it. I guess I can never get across the fact that all I want to do is act. For the last three years of my MGM contract I literally begged for straight acting roles. I just got one, *A Woman's Face*, and that did very much all right at the box office, too. But immediately I was put back in the clothes horse roles, where I simply walked around with egg on my face, doing nothing.[68]

Joan Crawford would continue to consider *Humoresque* to be one of the best films of her long career.

John Garfield plays Paul Boray, a concert violinist who is filled with alternate doses of ambition and bitterness. Joan Crawford is Helen Wright, a wealthy woman who sponsors Paul but falls in love with him and is tortured by her feelings for him. While Paul exhibits some attraction to her, he also maintains an attraction to Gina (Joan Chandler), a fellow musician he met when first learning how to play with an orchestra. From that point the film is a study in contrasts. Paul's natural talent and

---

67 Lid Off in Garfield Break with Warners. *The Los Angeles Times*. September 10, 1945
68 Louella Parsons Column. International News Service. October 20, 1945

John Garfield plays a concert violinist in Humoresque.

ambition is clouded by his confused feelings for both Gina and Helen, who are complete opposites as people and their impact on Paul's life and career. Paul's love for Helen is further thwarted by the fact that she is married, and struggling through a loveless marriage. Paul's parents, especially his long-supportive mother, are unsettled by his relationship with Helen. Paul's mother angrily confronts him. She even slaps him. Helen visits the mother, who confronts her, angrily expressing her dismay at the relationship while Helen tries hard to convince her that she loves Paul. Tortured and tormented, a weeping Helen walks the beach at night and finally decides to drown herself. Devastated, Paul is also determined and decides to continue with his music.

A consistent presence throughout the story is Oscar Levant as Paul's loyal friend Sid Jeffers. Paul first meets Jeffers when he's a boy and first sets his sights on a violin, which he wants as a birthday present. Sid plays piano in the Variety Store where Paul sees the violin, and connects with the boy's fascination with the instrument. Throughout the film, Sid exhibits wisdom, an acerbic sense of humor, and consistent support. It is a very complex character despite it being clearly in support, and makes an impact.

John Garfield is able to tap into a lot of his many abilities with the Nick character. Initially, Nick as a young man is bitter. He overhears his family talking about how useless he is not working and bringing money home during the Depression, instead spending his days rehearsing and perfecting his violin playing. It is his mother who defends him against the misgivings of the family, just as it was she who insisted his father buy him an $8 violin rather than a $2 toy. Thus, it would stand to reason that, years later, it is his mother who steps up to protect him from what she believes are the cynical wiles of a rich woman.

The father responds with a character progression, gradually becoming more impressed with Nick's accomplishment as he becomes more successful. He doesn't notice factors beyond his son's success, which has overpowered his initial skepticism.

With a character who was cynical, bitter, driven, ambitious, sensual, and forceful, John Garfield's consistent presence as central to the film's narrative is very commanding. Thus, the fact that Joan Crawford is given top billing for a supporting role does not put Garfield's performance in a subordinate position, even though Crawford offers some of her career-best work.

The scenes of Nick playing violin were shot very convincingly, despite the fact that Garfield didn't play violin himself. Another significant factor to his performances is the attitude he presented in some of his early scenes with the orchestra. He projects a brashness that isn't normally seen in the other players. This attitude is what captivates Helen when she first meets him at the party.

John Garfield's method approach was not a problem for the much different style of acting that Joan Crawford utilized. Crawford had been married to method actor Franchot Tone, and connected cheerfully with his likeminded theater-based crowd. Crawford would continue to recall John Garfield as one of her best male co-stars.

What is most striking about *Humoresque* is director Jean Negulesco's keen visual sense. Initially this was difficult for Joan Crawford, who was used to working closely with the director and getting some guidance as to her performance within the context of his cinematic vision. But Negulesco was the type to sit back and let the actor find his or her own way. Realizing this conflicted with what Crawford was more comfortable with, artist Negulesco then drew some pictures of how he saw Helen, and this helped with Joan Crawford's interpretation of the role. Jean Negulesco's background as an artist serves him especially well in his filming of Helen's despondent walk on the beach, eventual suicide, and its aftermath. Expansive overhead wide shots, showing Helen staggering alone, surrounded by negative space, is briefly disrupted by a man walking his dog past her. Negulesco shoots a tight closeup of Crawford's face, and the cuts to the dangerous waves crashing on the shore. Moving the camera toward them, we almost feel Helen's drowning from her perspective. He then cuts to the confused dog walker who wonders how the woman he just saw suddenly disappeared and realizes what happened.

John Garfield and Joan Crawford light up the screen in Humoresque.

Everything in the sequence has its purpose. He cuts back from another shot of the waves to the shore, in the cold light of day, with a despondent Nick staring out, and being once again consoled by Sid. The last shot of Nick walking up the familiar New York street to his parents' store wraps the proceedings perfectly.

There's something that is very abstract about how the collection of shots come together in that scene that makes it beautiful, accentuated by how it cuts between scenes of Nick performing a concert that Helen was supposed to attend. The music is very powerful. Notably, at this point in the film, Helen has given Nick up because of his music; she recognizes that even though he loves her she will always take second place to his work.

While *Humoresque* furthered the resurgence in Joan Crawford's career at Warners that had begun with *Mildred Pierce*, it was the end of John Garfield's contract with the studio he had been with since his film debut in 1938. Now a veteran screen star, Garfield wanted greater creative control over the remainder of his career. He joined up with producer Bob Roberts and formed Enterpirse Productions, which allowed for independent deals that Garfield would orchestrate himself with various studios.

The post-war era found most Americans wanting to get back to normal life, and enjoy the country's jobs and prosperity by building suburbs and starting families. Meanwhile, unrest in various unions extended to the Screen Actors Guild, and John Garfield's liberal politics were aroused, even though, in a calculated move, he sided with the more conservative forces as he entered independent production. Garfield intended to make good films that not only offered a strong story, but also wanted to make a statement. According to his biography:

> He said he didn't want to turn movies into a lecture platform, but "there's fear in Hollywood about tackling dangerous subjects, difficult subjects ... I owe it to myself to be available when some enterprising people want to try something tough." Oh, he would still do commercial stuff to retain his commodity value at the box office. But he mainly wanted the kind of picture that would be harder to do but might turn out more interesting. (Garfield's) friends expected him to take a pratfall. Some thought he would be undone by his faith in Bob Roberts, whom they saw as a parasite – a hanger-on and one-man Garfield entourage.[69]

Initially considering a film version of Edgar Allen Poe's *The Tell-Tale Heart*, Garfield dropped that idea and pursued a script by Abraham Polonsky about prizefighting called *Body and Soul*.

---

69 Swindell, Larry. *Body and Soul: The Story of John Garfield.* NY: Morrow. 1975

BODY AND SOUL

Directed by Robert Rossen
Screenplay by Abraham Polonsky
Produced by Bob Roberts
Cinematography by James Wong Howe
Edited by Robert Parrish

Cast:
John Garfield, Lili Palmer, Hazel Brooks, Anne Revere, William Conrad, Joe Pevney, Lloyd Gough, Canada Lee, James Burke, Joe Devlin, Mary Currier, Artie Dorrell, Wheaton Chambers, George Tyne, Virginia Gregg, Glen Lee, John Indrisano, Sheldon Jett, Milton Kibbee, Cyril Ring, Art Smith, Tim Ryan, Peter Virgo, Shimen Ruskin, Larry QAnzalone, Ceferino Garcia, Frank Riggi, Ulysses William, Steve Benton, Eddie Borden Paul Bradley, James Carlisle, Herschel Graham, Wilbur Mack, Pat McKee, Harold Miller, Larry Steers, Sailor Vincent, Al Bain, Stuart Hall, Ted Lorch, Sid Melton, Forbers Murray, Paul Power, Bert Stevens, Sid Troy, Goerge M. Carleton, Al Eben, Sayre Dearing, Joe Gray, Mike Lally, George Magrill, William H. O'Brien, Mike Ragan, Bob Reeves, Dan Tobey, John Wald.

Released November 11, 1947
Enterprise Productions for United Artists
Running time: 104 minutes
Black and White

Now acting as his own producer, John Garfield was able to choose projects that interested him. However, aside from that, Garfield could also explore areas of his ability that inspired him creatively, not just a job in a movie project the studio chose for him.

Garfield carefully selected what he considered the best people for the project, and surrounded himself with like-minded actors and filmmakers who believed in the same purpose. Robert Rossen was a screenwriter Garfield had been fond of at Warners (he wrote *Dust Be My Destiny* and *Out of the Fog* and co-wrote the screenplay for *The Sea Wolf*). Rossen had directed one film (*Johnny O'Clock*) from his own script and was eager to explore directing further. Anne Revere, Lloyd Gough, and Canada Lee were notable leftist actors.

Garfield had not played a boxer since *They Made Me a Criminal* eight years earlier and, now closing in on 35 years of age, was considered a bit old to play a street punk whose natural fighting ability transforms him into a heavyweight fighter. Plus, the story was already formulaic. A meteoric rise, a change in the fighter's attitude where he forgets people from his past, gangsters who become a part of his immediate world that result in big money, etc. But Garfield also saw in the script enough statements of purpose to make the material appealing. He saw that the central character was genuine, and saw the mother character as an anchor, but also that the quest of money was destructive. Those are the themes and issues that stood out to Garfield from Abraham Polonsky's script, which was originally called *The Burning Desire*.

The story is told in flashback. John Garfield plays Charley Davis, a middleweight boxing champion, who wakes up yelling the name "Ben" then flees from his training quarters to his mother's home, telling her that this "Ben" died that day. His mother, cold and bitter, tells him he should leave. When he sees his ex-girlfriend Peg, she falls to her bed and weeps. Charley then ends up at a club where another ex-girlfriend, Alice, is performing. He drinks and looks back on his life and career. He is reminded

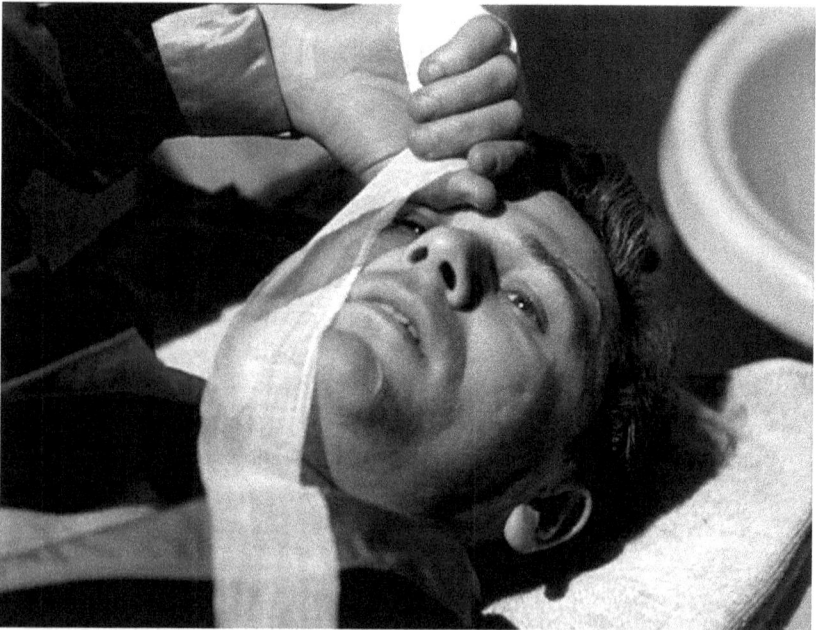

John Garfield is a reflective prizefighter who is in deep with the mob in Body and Soul.

of when a bomb is thrown into a speakeasy and causes his parents' nearby store to explode, killing his father. This leads him to enter the fight game, because his mother (Anne Revere) needs money and he is insulted when a welfare agent visits and interviews her for charity qualification. Charley also meets Peg Born (Lilli Palmer), a painter in Greenwich Village and they fall in love. Charley wins his first few fights, arranged by a promoter named Quinn (William Conrad) with support from his old friend Shorty (Joe Pevney) whom Charley considers his manager. A championship bout is arranged between Charley and a black fighter, Ben Chaplin (Canada Lee), who holds the welterweight title. Ben has a blood clot near his brain and has been told to retire, but the promoters, including mobster Roberts (Lloyd Gough), who runs the boxing racket in New York, tell Ben's and his manager that they have arranged for the fight to be an easy one that goes to a decision, which he will lose. Charley, however, is not told of this, and boxes aggressively as usual. An angry Shorty later reveals to Charley that Ben was sick. Charley is upset, but Roberts is now in control. This upsets Shorty, who realizes he has been phased out and leaves the club. He is attacked by one of Roberts' henchmen, but Charley comes out and rescues him. A dazed and angry Shorty then staggers into the street, is hit by a car, and killed. Peg then realizes that she must give Charley an ultimatum – quit boxing or she will quit him. Charley chooses boxing and continues to achieve money and fame, becoming more involved with Alice and being more reckless with his money. One good thing he does is ask Ben to take Shorty's place and be his manager. Charley's next fight, however, is a fix. Roberts insists that he throw a fight, in a decision, to a newcomer named Jackie Marlowe. Ben tries to convince Charley not to throw the fight. Roberts hears him and fires him, but Ben angrily refuses to leave unless Charley himself says he must. In a rage, Ben starts swinging his fits and falling until he finally drops dead. Charley goes into the fight with Marlowe, and they carry each other for several rounds, much to the chagrin of the bored crowd. Marlowe then unloads on Charley, pummeling him until the round ends. Charley realizes he is part of the same type setup that happened to Ben Chaplin. An unnerved Charley answers the bell with the same aggression and ends up winning with a knockout. Roberts confronts him as he leaves the ring, and Charley states, "What are you going to do, kill me? Everybody dies." He reconnects with a happy Peg, as he chooses to now leave prizefighting.

The structure of this film is significant in that we are first introduced to Charley at the end, after he has risen up, made great money, allowed negative influences to permeate his world in order to achieve success,

Promoter William Conrad makes a deal with prizefighter John Garfield who is supported by his buddy Joe Pevney in Body and Soul.

and watched people with honesty and integrity die (from his father to Ben Chaplin). As we look back and see Charley's rise, realizing his fall is to happen, we understand his perspective. John Garfield had, by now, offered some exceptional acting in many different films, but in *Body and Soul* he presents a character so complex and fascinating, it laid the groundwork for latter day actors from James Dean and Marlon Brando to Robert DeNiro and Al Pacino.

There are some essential factors in this independent production that would likely not have happened if the project were made for a major studio. First, the character of Charley is significantly Jewish, not a nondescript character with no discernible ethnicity. Also, rather than present an African American actor in a tangential or subservient role, Canada Lee is allowed to tap into his innate acting skills with an emotionally charged performance that truly resonates. Lee jokingly told the press: "When I'm acting, they say I'm, a good fighter, and when I'm fighting, they say I'm a good actor."[70] And the idea of making a lot of money, while attractive to Charley, does not impress his stoic mother. "I'm beautiful," says the plain-featured woman, "why would I want to be rich?"

That Garfield insisted on using noted left leaning actors who were already being watched by the House Un-American Activities Committee (they had been compiling a dossier on Garfield since the early 1940s) was another courageous move. Canada Lee was actually a former boxer, who quit the ring in 1932 after his eyesight became problematic. He began

---

70   Erskine Johnson column. *Los Angeles Daily News.* January 8, 1947

John Garfield as the prizefighter who tries hard to reason with his mother Anne Revere in Body and Soul.

his acting career on Broadway two years later. His Civil Rights activism and connection with noted progressives like Langston Hughes and Paul Robeson was becoming a problem by the time Garfield asked for him to play in *Body and Soul.* By 1949, Lee's blacklist was so extreme he was told to denounce Robeson as a communist. Lee refused. He worked in some films overseas, notably *Cry The Beloved Country* (1951), and died in 1952.

Anne Revere was an active member of the Communist Party by the time she did this film, and refused to cooperate with the House Un-American Activities Committee, resulting in her 1951 appearance in *A Place in the Sun* to be her last until nearly 20 years later. She would appear again in John Garfield's next movie, *Gentlemen's Agreement* for which she would receive an Oscar nomination.

Lloyd Gough's wife, actress Karen Morely, was blacklisted the same year *Body and Soul* was released, and Gough was in 1951, both for not cooperating with the House Un-American Activities Committee. Gough returned to the Broadway stage, and returned to film in the 1960s when cast by friend Frank Sinatra in *Tony Rome* (1967) and later as a regular on TV's *The Green Hornet.* Gough remained active well into the 1970s, including an appearance in the blacklist drama *The Front* (1976).

Body and Soul is often lauded as a well-directed, visually stimulating, dramatically compelling boxing drama, among the very best of its kind. Only some assessments of the film address the film's message about the quest for more money being fraught with misdirection and corruption. The fact that the film opens with Charley at rock bottom, and ends back in real time with him realizing he has been duped in the same manner by promoters, adds to the structural impact of the narrative. His opponent is young and brash, as Charley had been, so in fighting back and winning the bout, Charley is defeating the negative aspects of the man he once was. His quitting the fight game and embracing Pat, the only moral compass that is still in his life, offers a happy ending in spite of the darkness of the story.

Garfield's canny choice of James Wong Howe as cinematographer resulted in the creative idea to shoot the boxing sequences with a handheld camera while on roller skates. While these shots were carefully edited into the action, they added to the rhythm of the boxing sequences

Cinematographer James Wong Howe films a fight scene with a hand held camera while on roller skates in Body and Soul.

that also included quick cutaways to closeups of sweaty determined faces. The final fight is quite mesmerizing. It looks and feels a lot grittier than most boxing movie scenes, in part thanks to the hand-held cinematography. It's easy to see how this film influenced later boxing movies that are now much more well-known and widely seen; somebody watching *Body and Soul* today might find some of its tropes tired, but this is actually the foundation, or one of the foundations, for the boxing subgenre.

Body and Soul was a hit with both audiences and critics, John Garfield's first venture into independent cinema achieving the success he desired. *The New York Times* stated:

> After all the assorted prizefight pictures that have been paraded across the screen—after all the pugs and muggs and chorus girls and double-crosses and last-round comebacks that we've seen— it hardly seemed likely that another could possibly come along with enough zing and character to it to captivate and excite us for two hours. Yet *Body and Soul* has up and done it, with interest and excitement to spare, and we heartily recommend it. Trim, taut and full of vitality, Mr. Garfield really acts like a fresh kid who thinks the whole world is an easy set-up—until the fates close inexorably in, until the wraps are ripped from his illusions and he finds himself owned, body and soul. It is Canada Lee, however, who brings to focus the horrible pathos of the cruelly exploited prizefighter. As a Negro ex-champ who is meanly shoved aside, until one night he finally goes berserk and dies slugging in a deserted ring, he shows through great dignity and reticence the full measure of his inarticulate scorn for the greed of shrewder men who have enslaved him, sapped his strength and then tossed him out to die.[71]

While there are many great performances in John Garfield's filmography, there are roughly a dozen that truly define his work as an actor. *Body and Soul* may very well present him at his career best. From this point, the success of his first indie film venture meant that John Garfield could go where he wanted creatively, choosing projects that mattered to him and made statements that he believed were important.

Interestingly enough, *Body and Soul* generated some controversy when one of the video versions was discovered to be missing ten seconds. According to J. Hoberman:

> Annette Insdorf, Columbia professor and the author of *Indelible Shadows, the first history of film and the Holocaust,* forwarded me

---

71 Body and Soul review. *The New York Times.* November 10, 1947

an email she had received from Chicago Police Officer Maurice Richards, regarding an apparent cut in the DVD he had recently purchased of *Body and Soul*. "It isn't the money, it's his way of showing," the delivery man says when Charlie guiltily advises him that betting is foolish. The next 20 words -- "In Europe, the Nazis are killing people like us just because of their religion. But here, Charlie Davis is champion"—are gone, leaving only his final statement, "and we are proud." The omission, Lt. Richards wrote, is "disgraceful, outrageous and deliberate. The anti-Nazi content and speaking out against the Holocaust has been purposefully removed from the film. New generations of viewers will never be able to see and appreciate the true legacy of this great work of art and Jewish heritage." He further called for a "thorough investigation" of the deletion: "It is important to find out when, by whom, and if possible, why this was done." Prof. Insdorf made a number of inquiries on the lieutenant's behalf. Eventually, Patricia Hanson, of the American Film Institute, figured out that Republic Pictures Home Video had released two VHS versions of *Body and Soul*; the 1986 version included the complete dialogue while a 1992 "45th anniversary edition" (advertised as "digitally remastered from the original") did not and was identical to the Artisan Home Entertainment DVD purchased by Lt. Richards. "Because of various controversies surrounding the film," she noted, "it is very likely that the cut was made on the master decades ago." The most reasonable explanation for the cut was given to me by Dave Kehr, the extremely knowledgeable film critic. The 1992 version was likely remastered from an export negative. Pointing out that a small studio like Enterprise had no overseas distribution, he theorized that whoever had licensed the movie from Enterprise in the late '40s cut their negative out of deference to the West German market.[72]

Later blu ray versions of *Body and Soul* are complete and contain the ten seconds of dialog cut by just one of the VHS distributors.

Before he began another indie movie for his production company, John Garfield accepted a role in a promising story about anti-Semitism. And while he would not be cast in the lead, Garfield felt the project was significant enough to take an important supporting role.

---

72   Hoberman, J. The Jewish Brando. *Tablet*. March 3, 2013

GENTLEMAN'S AGREEMENT

Directed by Elia Kazan
Screenplay by Moss Hart based on the novel by Laura Z. Hobson
Produced by Darryl F. Zanuck
Cinematography by Arthur C. Miller
Edited by Harmon Jones

Cast:
Gregory Peck, Dorothy McGuire, John Garfield, Celeste Holm, Anne Revere, June Havoc, Albert Dekker, Jane Wyatt, Dean Stockwell, Nicholas Joy, Sam Jaffe, June Havoc, Albert Dekker, Jane Wyatt, Harold Vermilyea, Ransom M. Sherman, Curt Conway, Victor Kilian, Kathleen Lockhart, Louise Lorimer, Howard Negley, Roy Roberts, Frank Wilcox, Ed Argesti, Moran Farley, Edward Biby, Jane Earle, Louise Buckley, Jarry Denny, Patricia Cameron, Irene Dehn, Tom Coleman, Tom Handley, Joe Haworth, Franklyn Farnum, Jack Conrad, Virginia Gregg, Jane Green, Wilton Graff, Grace Field, Frank Godoy, Helen Gerald, Carl Leviness, Mauritz Hugo, George Leigh, Boyd Irwin, Gustave Lax, Robert Karnes, Raymond Largay, Lewis Leverett, Stella Rae, Herbert Ratner, Ken Lynch, Wilbur Mack, Gene Nelson, Mary Worth, Pattie Robbins, Frank Wilcox, Edwin Rochelle, Jesse White, Paul Russell, Robert Warick, Laura Treadwell, Amzie Strickland, Larry Steers, Wallace Scott.

Released November 11, 1947 (NY premiere), March, 1948 (wide release)
20th Century Fox
Running time: 118 minutes
Black and White

Gentleman's Agreement is based on a novel confronting anti-Semitism by Laura Z. Hobson, that had initially been serialized in *Cosmopolitan*. Hobson, who was Jewish, wrote the story when congressman John Rankin called columnist Walter Winchell a Jewish slur, and nobody in the House of Representatives condemned him for it. President of 20th Century Fox, Darryl F. Zanuck, was inspired for his studio to make a movie version of the story when he was banned from joining a restricted country club for being Jewish. In fact, Zanuck was not Jewish. But he realized in the situ-

Trade ad for Gentleman's Agreement.

ation that he couldn't bring himself to admit this to the club, thinking of his Jewish friends and colleagues.

Zanuck was warned not to make the movie. His Jewish colleagues stated that it would just stir up more trouble, now that the House Un-American Activities Committee was giving a lot of attention to movies and the new medium of television. But Zanuck insisted on going ahead with the project. Gregory Peck accepted the lead role against the advice of his agent, fearing that it would disrupt or might even end his promising career. The result was one of the highest grossing films of the year, which won several awards, including an Oscar for Best Picture.

However, in a book concentrating on the work of John Garfield, the perspective has to be regarding his contribution to the film. *Gentleman's Agreement* is not a John Garfield movie. He has a supporting role that is important, but his character doesn't even show up until roughly halfway through the feature.

The story deals with Philip Schuyler Green (Gregory Peck), a widowed writer who is assigned to explore and reveal anti-Semitism by pretending to be Jewish, and realizing the situations first hand. He meets his editor's pretty niece, Kathy Lacey (Dorothy McGuire) at a party and they start dating. Green discovers that Kathy had the original idea for the story. But when she finds out his approach, she is unsettled and begins to real-

A racial slur causes a confrontation. Gregory Peck, Celeste Holm, John Garfield, and Robert Karnes in Gentleman's Agreement.

ize her own acquiescence to the abject bigotry of others. The film deals with Green's confrontations and realizations, from his son Tommy (Dean Stockwell) being accosted for being Jewish, to the way opportunities and advantages that he had once taken for granted, are removed.

John Garfield's contribution is as Dave Goldman, an ominous presence, a veritable conscience, because he is a friend of Green's who happens to actually be Jewish. Garfield plays Dave as a happy, carefree sort, not with any chip on his shoulder like past characters who were troubled by their status. He is supportive of what Phil is trying to do, and his approach, and we are made to realize he has been fighting this battle quite naturally and for a long time.

Garfield's strongest scene is when Kathy and Phil split up after Tommy comes home crying after being shunned by his playmates and called racial slurs. Kathy hugs the child and reminds him "it's not true, you're no more Jewish than I am." Kathy doesn't realize that it is the slurs themselves that are offensive, and not because they are misdirected at one who is not Jewish (which goes back to Zanuck's experience and his inspiration for producing the movie). This causes the breakup, and later we find Kathy in a restaurant and Dave meeting her there. She tells Dave about having gone to a dinner party earlier in the evening where a man named Lockhart told an offensive ethnic joke and while nobody laughed, they also remained quiet and allowed it to happen. Kathy says the experience sickened her. Dave says to Kathy:

> I wonder if you'd feel so sick if you had nailed him. There's a funny kind of elation about socking back. I learned that a long time ago. Phil's learned it. Lots of things are pretty rough, Kathy. This is just a different kind of a war. A man told a story at a dinner table, and the nice people didn't laugh. They even despised him for it, sure. But they let it pass. And what about the rest of the dinner guests? They're supposed to be on your side.

An example of Dave socking back is presented earlier in the film, when called a Jewish slur by a belligerent soldier in a club. Kathy realizes why she and Phil had the conflict, and they end up back together. But meanwhile, Phil had connected with co-worker Anne Dettrey (Celeste Holm) who says to him, regarding hypocrites:

> They scold Bilbo[73] and think they've fought the good fight for democracy in this country. They haven't got the guts to go from talking to action. One little action on one little front. Sure, I know it's not the whole answer, but it's got to start somewhere, and it's got to start with passion. Not pamphlets, not even your series. It's got to be with people. Rich people, poor people, big and little people. And it's got to be quick.

A romance seems imminent between the two characters, but Green realizes it is Kathy he loves, even though he wishes she had the same attitude as Anne.

The film was controversial, but well received. In its rave review, the show business trade magazine *Variety* stated, in part:

> The spectacular critical, popular and financial success of Laura Z. Hobson's Gentleman's Agreement as a novel should be repeated by Darryl F. Zanuck's brilliant and powerful film version. Just as the original story of the writer (character), who poses as a Jew to write a magazine series on anti-Semitism was a milestone in modern fiction, the picture is one of the most vital and stirring and impressive in Hollywood history. It should clean up at the boxoffice and bring deserved acclaim to its creators. The film is, if anything, an improvement over the novel. This is not merely because the story has been better focused and somewhat con-

---

73 A Mississippi governor of the time who was proudly racist.

densed, without softening the treatment. It is also more graphic and atmospheric than the book and, more importantly, because it has greater dramatic depth and force, and more personal, emotional impact. Even the least-informed and least-sensitive filmgoer can hardly fail to identify himself with the characters on the screen, and be profoundly moved. The picture provides an almost overwhelming emotional experience and thus is not only highly topical, but truly universal. John Garfield is a natural in the part of Dave, giving it admirable strength and understated eloquence.[74]

However not everyone was as enthused. Liberal writer Ring Lardner said, "The movie's moral is that you should never be mean to a Jew, because he might turn out to be a gentile."

While it is not essentially a John Garfield movie, his supporting role in a film as courageous (for its time) as *Gentleman's Agreement* has a significance regarding where it is placed in his career; right at the time he began doing independent projects where his own voice and perspective could be presented. And this wasn't a mere cameo like his brief stints in *Thank Your Lucky Stars, Daisy Kenyon,* or *Jigsaw.* Even though the film doesn't explore this in depth because Garfield's character isn't the main subject, it's interesting that we learn that Dave, despite being a soldier coming home from the war, is having a hard time finding housing because so many places are restricted to him. As stated earlier in the chapter, Garfield doesn't play Dave like he has a chip on his shoulder, but he is definitely wise to the prejudices he has had to face and has a tough streak that comes out when he needs to defend himself against them. Also notable is the tone of Garfield's voice in a scene after the incident with Tommy and the breakup with Kathy, where he tells Phil that they got him with his kid, and that's about the worst they can do. More than any other time in the movie, Garfield makes Dave sound resigned and maybe a bit bitter.

Gentleman's Agreement sometimes feels flat today in that it only explores the temporary effects of anti-Semitism on a person who is upper-middle class; Phil isn't having to struggle with finding a job, or a place to live, or to be treated even more poorly because he is a member of the working class. But a lot of the conversations surrounding prejudice, especially the way so many other people won't speak out even when they don't agree with what they're hearing or seeing, even though they can be a bit preachy, are still moving and relevant today, and can be apply to all forms of prejudice and racism.

---

74 Gentleman's Agreement review. *Variety.* November 11, 1947

John Garfield was now ready to return to independent productions with his own company, and his next film for enterprise, *Force of Evil*, continued to arouse the negative interest of the House Un-American Activities Committee. The HUAC had held their first hearings in late 1947 naming the following ten individuals as Communist : Alvah Bessie, Herbert Biberman, Lester Cole, Edward Dmytryk, Ring Lardner, Jr., John Howard Lawson, Albert Maltz, Samuel Ornitz, Adrian Scott, and Dalton Trumbo. Roy Brewer of the Motion Picture Industry Council was interviewed in October of 1947 when he claimed he knew 13 writers, directors, and actors who were involved in Communist activities. Among those, he included John Garfield.

FORCE OF EVIL

Directed by Abraham Polonsky
Screenplay by Polonsky and Ira Wolfert based on the novel by Wolfert
Produced by Bob Roberts
Cinematography by George Barnes
Edited by Arthur Seid

Cast:
John Garfield, Thomas Gomez, Marie Windsor, Howland Chamberlain, Roy Roberts, Paul Fix, Stanley Prager, Barry Kelley, Paul McVey, Beatrice Pearson, Georgia Backus, Jan Dennis, Bob Stebbins, Ann Duncan, Charles Evans, Perry Ivins, Milton Kibbee, Jack Overman, Frank Pharr, Tim Ryan, Esther Somers, Barbara Wooddell, Sid Tomack, Murray Alper, John Collum, Jesse Arnold, Roger Cole, Sam Ash, Cliff Clark, Margert Bret, Larry Blake, Roger Cole Jim Drum, Jimmee Dundee, Carl Hanson, Estelle Etterre, Sherry Hall, Chuck Hamilton, Richard Elmore, David Fresco, Ray Hirsch, Paul Frees, Bert Hanlon, Paul Newlan, Will Lee, John Indrisano, Bill Neff, Jack Lambert, Forbes Murray, William H. O'Brien, Carl Sklover, Louise Saraydar, Cap Somers, Robert B. Williams, Phil Tully, Esther Somers, Barbara Stone, Harry Wilson, Diane Stewart, Brick Sullivan, Max Wagner, Joe Warfield, Robert Strong,

Released December 25, 1948 (NY premiere), March, 1949 (wide release)
Enterprise Productions and Roberts Productions for MGM
Running time: 79 minutes
Black and White

Setting up his second independent production, a screen version of the novel *Tucker's People*, John Garfield, along with Bob Roberts, took a chance on giving screenwriter Abraham Polonsky his first directing job. According to Phillip Scheuer in *The Los Angeles Times*:

> It took Hollywood five years to lick the story of *Tucker's People*, but they finally did, and the picture went before cameras last week. Three of the men who whipped it into filmable form were responsible for last year's box-office KO *Body and Soul*. Bob Roberts, the producer; John Garfield, the actor, and Abraham Polonsky, whose original screen play of *Body and Soul* won him

an Academy award nomination. Ira Wolfert, author of the novel of *Tucker's People*, collaborated with Polonsky on the script. "The book was essentially cynical and defeatist," Polonsky said last week. ."Wolfert felt that, too; the war had changed his view. So our picture will show Joe Morse (Garfield) as a corporation lawyer who rediscovers not only his responsibility in life but also his soul. At the close he pulls down the world of evil he has helped create with him; it is a visible act of regeneration. "This is not a gangster picture, but a psychological study of men's 'business' relations to a racket. Morse, Tucker and the others would have liked to see lotteries legalized; meanwhile they succumbed to corruption." Now, he added a trifle cynical himself, policy banks flourish once again and men are still trying to have them legalized. Polonsky, with Wolfert, prepared such a complete and comprehensive shooting script, down to the last angle, cut and word, that Roberts and Garfield permitted him to take over the direction as well. It is his first time behind the camera.[75]

John Garfield gathered the best people he could find and went into production on a fast-talking, compelling crime drama that once again offered one of the actor's finest performances.

John Garfield plays Joe Morse, a lawyer working for a gangster, Ben Tucker (Roy Roberts). Tucker wants to control the numbers racket in New York, and that means little guys with smaller operations will be swallowed up and go out of business. Joe's brother Leo (Thomas Gomez) runs one of the smaller operations. While both brothers are tainted with corruption, Joe is supportive of Leo, but Leo looks negatively toward Joe. Leo made sacrifices to help put Joe through law school, and does not like how deeply into corruption his work has taken him. Where Joe is smooth and in control, Leo is tense and blustery, with a myriad of health problems as a result. Joe arranges for Leo's place to get raided by police, and then goes to the jail, pays their fines, and gets them released, including Leo, his timid bookkeeper Freddy Bauer (Howard Chamberlain), and his young secretary Doris Lowry (Beatrice Peason). As planned, on the 4th of July when most numbers players pick the number 776, the number hits and the small businesses are bankrupted, allowing Tucker to take over. Leo realizes, against his better judgement, he must now align with Tucker, and Joe protects him, not allowing the nervous Bauer to quit. Joe is informed by Leo's wife (Marie Windsor) that Leo's phone is tapped. Bauer calls the new D.A. and turns Leo in to get himself out. He is also confronted by a man named Wally (Stanley Prager), who works for

75 Scheuer, Phillip K. Tucker's People. *Los Angeles Times*. June 13, 1948

John Garfield plays corrupt lawyer Joe Morse in the daring film Force of Evil.

Tucker's rival Ficco (Paul Fix) and wants information. Joe is determined, but also pragmatic, and when Leo is kidnapped and dies while in custody, Joe realizes he must do something to redeem himself as a man.

It is interesting how thematically similar *Force of Evil* is to *Body and Soul*. In each film, John Garfield plays a character who connects with gangsters for a sure payoff and later wants to do what's right and save his soul. Each are dramas that feature characters seeking materialism and then redemption. And both raised the eyebrows of the House Un-American Activities Committee for their attacks on capitalism; taking broad themes, streamlining them, and placing them in the screenplay. It didn't help that Abraham Polonsky would tell the press that his screenplay was an "autopsy of capitalism."

John Garfield's performance is practically a culmination. The dialog is sharp and witty, and Garfield spits out his lines with a rhythm that makes them truly come to life. It isn't the same sort of line readings he gave as an angry young man in Warner Brothers potboilers. Joe Morse is not a street kid he is a savvy mouthpiece who understands the rackets. He is smart, cunning, but his ambition is such that he ruins his brother's life. He then seeks some sort of redemption.

Setting up a shot with John Garfield in Force of Evil.

Thomas Gomez turns in one of the finest performances of his career as brother Leo. Overweight, sweaty, and trembling with stressful anger, Gomez presents his character as focused, driven, but limited in success. His smooth younger brother has gone much further, but in comparison to Joe's gangster connections, Leo considers himself an honest business man.

Force of Evil is highlighted by newcomer Beatrice Pearson, a stage actress who only made two films (this is her first), choosing to concentrate on theater. Ms. Pearson's Doris is young and naïve, wanting to do what's best, not realizing the depth of Leo's activities, and mistrusting Joe while also being attracted to him. The magnetism of John Garfield's performance is the same as that which Joe Morse presents to Doris, whose attraction is against her better judgment. Joe and Doris have a revealing conversation in a taxi cab. Doris shows that she isn't actually naïve as perveived, when she talks about how magicians fooled her as a little girl because she paid attention to what they said and not what they did, but she knows better now. This is also the first time in the film where Joe starts to exhibit some guilt over his and Leo's situation.

Several characters perform activities with a reluctance, and a realization that what they are doing is technically not right, but is ultimately what seems best for advancement. Polonsky's vision as a director allowed for his screenplay's perspective to survive onto the finished film without augmentation. Polonksy thought Robert Rossen took his script for *Body and Soul* and made what is essentially a boxing picture. Polonsky made *Force of Evil* much more than a standard crime drama or film noir. David Thomson stated in *The New Republic*:

> What makes the film so uncommon and so much more than a noir melodrama is the way that controlled tension between criminal lowlifes and poetic talk is matched by the stylization of décor and action soaring above the elements of a crime film. The art direction was by the very talented Richard Day (his credits included *The Grapes of Wrath*, *How Green Was My Valley*, Fritz Lang's *Man Hunt*, and then later, *On the Waterfront*). The ambition in the film's look begins with a view of Trinity Church jammed between Wall Street towers and ends with metaphor as Joe descends endless steps beneath the George Washington Bridge to find a corpse in the river. Along the way, the film sees every staircase as a moral structure. This willful and self-conscious artistry has disturbed some viewers—they complain that it's not playing fair by the rules of film noir. But Polonsky's target was the structure of capitalism and the way the numbers racket was a mockery of the banking system.[76]

The location shooting in *Force of Evil* really grounds the story in a sense of time and place. The shot of Garfield descending the stairs is just beautiful; he even says he's going "down to the bottom of the earth." Martin Scorsese and others have cited this film as a major influence on their work and it's easy to see why with scenes like this one.

It has been stated that, during a break in filming, Abraham Polonksy took cinematographer George Barnes to an exhibition of Edward Hop-

---

76 Thomson, David. What is the Most Dangerous Film in History? *The New Republic.* July 29, 2012

per paintings and said: "This is how I want the movie to look." Imogen Sara Smith stated in *Bright Lights Film Journal*:

> This is not the glamorous noir world of trench-coated heroes and femme fatales, but a world of small-time crooks, struggling family men who happen to be on the wrong side of the law, cowards and losers and mean thugs. The lighting and camera-work by George Barnes were based on Edward Hopper's paintings, with wide shots of solitary figures moving through urban canyons, stark lamplight in nocturnal offices, and the beautifully bleak dawn light under the George Washington Bridge, where Joe goes to find his brother's body. Polonsky claimed this haunting final scene was not about moral redemption, merely revenge; but Joe's revenge is also against himself, a repudiation of his whole way of life.[77]

Not all of the highlights feature John Garfield. There is a particularly strong scene where Leo attempts to protect the meek Bauer who is especially nervous because he realizes the rival gangsters are coming for Leo. They sit in a diner as Bauer has arranged, and when Ficco's men descend upon the building, Leo accosts his supposed friend, asking "how could you do this to me?" Bauer flees and is shot to death. It is at that point when Leo is captured and dies while in custody.

However, John Garfield's character and performance dominate the narrative as he rumbles through the artful dialog with a sense of purpose that presents the depth of Joe Morse's complex personality. The semi-documentary style, with Garfield, as Morse, supplying the narration, emphasizes this focus.

Force of Evil was selected to the National Film Registry in 1994, and has lived on as not only a quintessential example of post-war film noir, but as a response to the House Un-American Activities Committee by filmmakers who were eventually blacklisted. However, the HUAC continued to monitor John Garfield and took special interest in his next project.

---

77 Smith, Imogen Sara. Plumbing the Depths of Capitalism in Force of Evil. *Bright Lights Film Journal.* July 31, 2008

WE WERE STRANGERS

Directed by John Huston
Screenplay by Huston and Peter Viertel based on the novel by Robert Sylvester
Produced by S.P. Eagle (Sam Spiegel)
Cinematography by Russell Metty
Edited by Al Clark

Cast:
John Garfield, Jennifer Jones, Pedro Armendáriz, Gilbert Roland, Ramon Novarro, Wally Cassell, David Bond, José Pérez, Morris Ankrum, Robert Tafur, Tito Renaldo, Loretta Russell, Helen Dickson, Peter Virgo, Frank Godoy, Roberta Hanyes, John Huston, Paulo Monte, Mimi Aguglia, Salvador Baguez, Argentina Brunetti, Charles Grannuci, Jack Clisby, Spencer Chan, Freddy Chapman, Richard Neill, George Nardell, Kay Kouri, King Lockwood, Sol Murgi, Julian Rivero, Paul Marion, Joel Rene, Santiago Martinez, Waclaw Rekwart, Alex McSweyen, Rodd Redwing, Tina Minard, Alex Montoya, Harry J. Vejar, Joe Sawaya, Thomas Quon Wo, Billy Wilson, Leonard Strong, Sammy Shack, Felipe Turich.

Released April 27, 1949
Columbia Pictures
Running time: 106 minutes
Black and White

During the filming of *Force of Evil* there was some publicity about its filmmakers entering into television production. An article in *The Los Angeles Times* stated:

> Roberts Productions, the John Garfield, Bob Roberts and Abraham Polonsky organization, plans to develop a television program of 28 half-hour subjects about 26 different American cities. First will be shot in New York while the company is filming *The Numbers Racket*, new and probably temporary title for *Tucker's People*. These subjects will be documentary impressions of each city and the people who have contributed most to its welfare during a certain period of time.[78]

---

78 Television Documentaries Planned. *The Los Angeles Times.* June 23, 1948

Instead, John Garfield accepted the male lead for *We Were Strangers* from John Huston, whose most recent films *The Treasure of the Sierra Madre* and *Key Largo*, were both major successes.

While he was filming *Key Largo*, John Huston made the decision to leave his home studio of Warner Brothers, much like John Garfield had a few years earlier, so he could make films without studio interference. Entering into independent production, calling his company Horizon Pictures, Huston wanted John Garfield for a lead role in a movie version of Robert Sylvester's novel *Rough Sketch*. Huston made arrangements with Garfield's production company, Enterprise, and Bob Roberts productions, to secure the actor to the project. Columbia Pictures agreed to be the distributor.

John Huston had originally wanted to cast John Garfield in *The Treasure of the Sierra Madre*, in the role that ended up going to Tim Holt. Garfield was interested, but was busy working on his own project at the time. Huston and Garfield shared similar political views, and *We Were Strangers* was very much in tune with those shared views, so the director got his actor, who was interested in playing the role.

John Garfield plays Tony Fenner, an American who is part of an anti-government group in Cuba, posing as someone looking for Cuban entertainers to perform in the USA. Jennifer Jones is China Valdez, who sees her brother shot to death because he distributes anti-government pamphlets. She witnesses the assassination and sees his assailant, Armando Ariete (Pedro Armendáriz). She vows to seek revenge by killing him herself, despite realizing what would then become of her. Fenner redirects her and requests that she join his group. Fenner discovers that China's family lives by a cemetery where a senior official has a family plot. He plans to assassinate that official, then dig a tunnel from China's home to the cemetery and plant a bomb to be detonated at the man's funeral, thus killing all the officials in attendance at the man's funeral. As the tunnel is being created, the workers ponder the fact that the bomb would also be killing innocents at the funeral. Once the tunnel is finished, an assassination of the official does take place, but it is discovered that the memorial will not be held at the cemetery as anticipated. Meanwhile, Ariete, who noticed China early in the film while she was working at a bank, continues to stalk her, jealous of her relationship with Fenner. China seethes angrily when he is around, holding in her desire to kill him for murdering her brother. Ariete reveals that Fenner was born in Cuba but she has fallen in love with him. When the plot fails, an angry Fenner prepares to leave Cuba, ruing the fact that he must face those who helped fund his trip without any

Trade ad for We Were Strangers.

results or accomplishment. However, Fenner refuses to leave Cuba without China. The result is violence, revolution, and, ultimately celebration.

Although it takes place in Cuba, *We Were Strangers* was shot on the Columbia Pictures studio lot with second unit work, featuring doubles,

John Garfield and Jennifer Jones in We Were Strangers.

filmed in Havana. Director John Huston believed in the project but was said to be distracted by some personal issues and not always concentrating on his work. A lot of the script was written during filming, and the original ending was rewritten by a studio-hired Ben Hecht without credit.

The review for *We Were Strangers* in *Modern Screen* was perhaps the most positive the film received:

> In my opinion this picture is a work of art. It tells of a group of Cuban revolutionists in the early 1930s when that island was rule by a dictator-president, and it seemed freedom had vanished to be replaced by machine guns. The six live together eating, talking, digging. They who had recently been strangers are now inhabitants of a private world. But there isn't room to tell the whole story. This is a picture that will exhaust you. It mixes moments of poetry with moments of nightmare. It is beautiful, and terrible, and the acting is all so magnificent there's no sense in even trying to single out any performer. See *We Were Strangers*, its like may not come your way again.[79]

However most reviews of *We Were Strangers* were unfortunately negative. *The Hollywood Reporter* denounced its politics: "a shameful hand-

---

79 We Were Strangers review. *Modern Screen.* May, 1949

book of Marxian dialectics ... the heaviest dish of Red theory ever served to an audience outside the Soviet."[80] Meanwhile, the Communist newspaper *The Daily Worker* called the film "capitalist propaganda."[81] *We Were Strangers* played theaters only briefly and was a box office flop. Now, in the 21st century, there are some film buffs who consider it an underrated masterpiece from John Huston.

We Were Strangers features a solid role that seemed to be made for Garfield considering his personal politics, and even though their romance in the film didn't have a lot of heat he and Jennifer Jones work well together. Unfortunately, they were both cast as Cubans when they are not, but it's notable that the film boasted a supporting cast made up of several great Latino actors, particularly Ramon Navarro. The digging of the tunnel is thrilling and suspenseful as we wait to see whether they will get caught or whether their plan will even work, and Armendáriz makes a great, sinister villain.

Meanwhile, the House Un-American Activities Committee continued its investigation into possible Communist activity in movies. According to John Garfield's biographer:

> After the first movement of its witch hunting symphony, the HUAC closed its show for a three-year intermission of fact finding. John Garfield was one of many solvent screen stars who, under advice of counsel, furnished the committee with a statement of loyalty to the United States government and a denial of association with Communists, thus hoping to hold the investigators at arm's length.[82]

John Garfield finished *We Were Strangers* and took a stage role in the Clifford Odets play *The Big Knife*. It had a trial run and then made it to Broadway, where it played for several weeks before Garfield returned to movies. After a three-month run on Broadway in *The Big Knife*, John Garfield closed the production to take a trip to Europe before appearing in the movie *Under My Skin*, for 20th Century Fox, based on the Ernest Hemingway short story *My Old Man*.

---

80 Gosse, Van. *Where the Boys are: Cuba, Cold War America and the Making of a New Left*. London: Verso, 1993

81 Auerbach, Jonathan *Dark Borders: Film Noir and American Citizenship*. Duke University Press. 2011

82 Swindell, Larry. *Body and Soul: The Story of John Garfield*. NY: Morrow. 1975

UNDER MY SKIN

Directed by Jean Negulesco
Screenplay by Casey Robinson from the short story *My Old Man* by Ernest Hemingway
Produced by Casey Robinson
Cinematography by Joseph LaShelle
Edited by Dorothy Spencer

Cast:
John Garfield, Micheline Presle, Luther Alder, Orley Lindgren, Noel Drayton, Paul Bryar, Ann Codee, Anthony George, Harry Martin, A.A. Merola, Joe Warfield, Dusty Anderson, Frank Arnold, Edward Biby, Eugene Borden, Peter Camin, Monique Chantal, Andre Charisse, Andre Charlot, Gordon B. Clarke, Charles De Ravenne, Wally Dean, Adolkph Faylauer, Lisa Ferrady, Elizabeth Flournoy, Steven Geray, Henry Herbert, Hans Hebert, Lee MacGregor, Enresto Molinari, Barry Norton, Peggy O'Connor, Jean Romaine, Milton Ryoce, Loulette Sablon, Maria Siletti, Beverly Thompson, Guy Zanette, Esteher Zeitlin

Released March 19, 1950
20th Century Fox
Running time: 86 minutes
Black and White

From the time John Garfield completed work on *Force of Evil*, producer Bob Roberts was considering several different properties in which he would star for his own production company, Enterprise. In an April, 1949 article, the press stated:

> Producer Bob Roberts, who has just returned from five weeks in New York during which he conferred about future plans with John Garfield. Garfield may appear in *Flight to Portabella* later, and is definite for *An American in Paris*, which Abraham Polonsky is writing abroad.

Of course this is not the same *An American in Paris* eventually filmed around the same time with Gene Kelly, as that story and screenplay was penned by Alan Jay Lerner.

The relationship between father and son was more prominent in the original story. Orley Lindgren and John Garfield in Under My Skin.

Another project about which Roberts, and Garfield, were quite serious, was *The Italian Story*, about the life of Italian orchestra conductor Guido Cantelli, and both sought out some locations while both were in Europe prior to the actor coming back to America to star in *Under My Skin*, which was originally titled *The Big Fall.*

One of the least known of all the John Garfield movies, *Under My Skin*, has quietly remained under the radar almost since its initial release in 1950. It has gotten little TV play and was never released to home video. On one hand this is unfortunate, because there are aspects of John Garfield's performance that exhibit a continued advancement in his work. But otherwise, this adaption of a 1922 Ernest Hemingway short story is a rather pale shadow of the original source material.

John Garfield plays Danny Arnold, a jockey who now rides in Italy because he can no longer get work in the United States after having thrown races in connection with gamblers. Danny is pressured by a gangster named Bork (Luther Adler) into throwing a race in Italy, but he refuses and then escapes to Paris with his son Joe (Orley Lindgren). He finds work there through his friend George Gardner (Noel Drayton), a British jockey. Bork catches up to Danny and threatens to kill him unless

The romance in Under My Skin *between Micheline Presle and John Garfield was an added distraction from the original story.*

he throws his next steeplechase race. He defies them, wins the race, but is killed in an accident at the finish line.

The point of the plot is that Danny wants to redeem himself for his son. But the narrative is distracted by a romance with Paule Manet, played by French actress Micheline Presle, who shares billing above the title with John Garfield. Danny first meets Paule at a café where she works, shortly after he arrives in Paris. Seeking the whereabouts of a friend, Paule informs Danny that the man was killed by gangsters for not paying a debt.

Under My Skin was shot in California, with second unit location filming done in Italy without the actors. Footage of racetracks at Auteuil, Chantilly, and Laffitte were shot during the summer of 1949 by an American crew headed by Norbert Brodine and Dewey Wrigley. Completing these scenes, Wrigley then took six cameras and a camera crew to the Merano racetrack in Italy. Dean Stockwell was considered for the job of playing Garfield's son, and the press announced it was going to be Bobby Driscoll, but neither ended up in the role. Micheline Presle was signed to a $40,000-per-film contract by 20th Century-Fox in August 1948. She was billed Prelle for this film, and her second movie for the studio, *American Guerrilla in the Philippines*.

Even though the Hemingway short story, *My Old Man*, was in the public domain, 20th Century Fox acquired the movie rights for $50,000 in January of 1949. Louella Parsons stated in her column:

> Ernest Hemingway's well-known story, *My Old Man* now belongs to 20th Century-Fox; Darryl Zanuck read it, and made an offer to buy it. Darryl will call it *The Big Fall*. He has John Garfield and Micheline Presle, France's number one movie actress, signed for the leads. This will be Micheline's first American picture. Garfield Is in Paris, and so is Casey Robinson, who will write the adaptation. Casey talked to John about the story, and it goes before the cameras when they are all home in Hollywood.[83]

Casey Robinson was a veteran screenwriter who started out doing titles for silent films like *The Patent Leather Kid* (1927) and *Bare Knees* (1928). Robinson had written the screenplays for such movie hits as *Captain Blood* (1935), *Dark Victory* (1939), *Now, Voyager* (1942), and, more recently, had written and produced another Hemingway adaption, *The Macomber Affair*. That success is what likely led him to this project. Jean Negulesco had already directed John Garfield in the films *Nobody Lives Forever* (1946) and *Humoresque* (1947).

Shooting began in September of 1949, and after filming had gone on for two weeks, John Garfield played a grueling game of tennis and suffered a heart attack. This caused production to shut down for three weeks while he recovered. Sheila Graham reported in her October 12th column:

> John Garfield called me from the Cedars of Lebanon Hospital to ask will I please correct the erroneous impression that his arteries are hardening "I tore a muscle in my heart," John tells me, "but after two weeks in bed I never felt totter in my life I'm also getting a new education. John Huston brought me the new *Don Quixote* translation and *Plato's Republic*. My wife has gone east to look after the kids again. The proves I'm better."[84]

But despite this, Garfield's performance is very strong and committed. He is given the opportunity to act with a youngster, and play a character that must deal with how his son perceives him, which gives him pause as

---

83 Louella Parsons Column. Hearst Syndicate. June 21, 1949
84 Sheila Graham Column. *Los Angeles Citizen Evening News*. October 12, 1949

to the activities in which he is engaging. Danny has been crooked so long he is simply inexperienced at doing the right thing. But his commitment to his son is such that he makes positive decisions despite the danger of the outcome.

By this point, John Garfield's screen character had changed a great deal since he made films like *Dust Be My Destiny* over ten years earlier. He is pragmatic rather than impulsive, concerned rather than bitter. Danny's experiences with gangsters in *Under My Skin* are violent ones. Earlier in the film, he tries to fight his way past three men who are trying to keep him from escaping, until the police arrive. Later on he is beaten into agreeing to throw a race which he ultimately refuses, and is sadly killed.

Following movies like *Force of Evil* and *We Were Strangers*, this movie doesn't feel as daring in its themes or its story. In some ways it feels like a bit of a step back for Garfield, but it is interesting to see him play against a child for most of the film, and play a father for the first time. One scene in particular that stands out occurs is the one right after Danny puts Joe on a train to America. Dan plays it cool, but when he turns away from the train and walks toward the camera, there are visible tears in his eyes. However, a lot of the scenes with Joe are kind of sentimental and dul. This is not the fault of Orley Lindgren, who did well with the role he was given and conveyed Joe's admiration for his father despite Danny's poor choices. Luther Adler, quite notably, is the actor who got the part of Joe Bonaparte in the original stage production of *Golden Boy* that Garfield coveted.

Some have considered the plot of *Under My Skin* to mirror John Garfield's troubles with the HUAC, a sort of "explanation" in the same manner as *On The Waterfront* was for Elia Kazan. But *Under My Skin* is really just a movie adaption of a solid Hemingway story that deals more specifically between father and son (Danny is called "Butler" in the short story). That it has an underlying theme of the central character's morality does not necessarily connect as specifically with John Garfield's problems with the HUAC.

Bosley Crowther in *The New York Times* noticed the flaws in this adaption of Hemingway's story in his review:

> The germ of a devastating drama which Ernest Hemingway conveyed in his story of a crooked jockey and his little boy under the title of *My Old Man* has been pretty well doused with anti-septics by Casey Robinson and Twentieth Century-Fox in a soggy romance based on that story and retitled *Under My Skin*. So much disinfective eye-wash has been blended into the tale that the consequent film is a limp and pallid affair. The Heming-

way yarn, you may remember, is a lean and guarded account of a youngster's idolatrous devotion to his obviously shady old man, who hangs around the horse parks of Europe because he has been banned from American tracks. And the whole cryptic irony of the story is that the old man never reforms, and the kid only gets a tiny glimmer of his crookedness after he has been killed in a steeplechase race. But in this vastly sugared dramatization the boy does discover that his dad is not only crooked but cruel, along about halfway through. And the rest of the picture is a fiction of how the jockey tries to make it up and redeem himself in his son's eyes, only to be killed accidentally in the end. Furthermore, the hard core of the story—the private love between the father and son, wholesomely and poignantly exclusive of the wicked and ruthless race track world—has been dissipated in this picture by the intrusion of a noble French dame who, in some manner not at all convincing, makes the devotion a three-way affair. No, we're afraid that Mr. Robinson, who wrote and produced the film, has expanded the Hemingway story into a characterless and meaningless romance.[85]

Under My Skin was not a success at the box office, and usually played as the second feature on double bills.

Bob Roberts continued to explore vehicles for John Garfield for independent production. *The Italian Story* negotiations eventually fizzled, but there were other movies being considered, including another announced Abraham Polonsky screenplay, *Port Afrique* based on a Bernard Dryer novel. Roberts also bought the rights to Nelson Algren's novel *The Man With The Golden Arm*, to star Garfield.

Ironically, perhaps, John Garfield's next movie venture was another screen version of an Ernest Hemingway story. Filmed before in 1944 as *To Have and Have Not* with Humphrey Bogart and Lauren Bacall, the version with John Garfield, *The Breaking Point* was, unlike *Under My Skin*, a much more faithful adaption of the original source material. Even more ironically, John Garfield signed a five-picture deal with his old studio Warner Brothers, with the understanding that he be allowed to continue making independent films for his own company.

---

85   Under My Skin review. *The New York Times*. March 18, 1950

THE BREAKING POINT

Directed by Michael Curtiz
Screenplay by Ranald MacDougal from the story *To Have and Have Not*
by Ernest Hemingway
Produced by Jerry Wald
Cinematography by Ted D. McCord
Edited by Alan Crosland Jr.

Cast:
John Garfield, Patricia Neal, Phyllis Thaxter, Juano Hernandez, Wallace
Ford, Edmond Ryan, Ralph Dumke, Guy Thomajan, William Campbell,
Sherry Jackson, Donna Jo Boyce, Victor Sen Yung, Paul Vierro, Helen
Hatch, Juan Hernandez, James Griffith, Alex Gerry, John Doucette, Glen
Turnbull, Paul McGuire, Bob MacLean, George Hoagland, John Alvin,
Dick Gordon, Chet Brandenburg, H.W. Gim, Peter Brocco, Mary Car-
roll, Norman Field, Juan Duvall, Spencer Chan, John Close, Len Hendry,
Glen Turnbull, Charles Horvath, Tommy Lee, Norman Phillips Jr. Jack
Mower, Benny Long, Beverly Mook, Robert B. Williams.

Released October 6, 1950
Warner Brothers
Running time: 97 minutes
Black and White

It all started when Howard Hawks told Ernest Hemingway on a fishing trip that he could make a good movie out of Hemingway's worst
book, citing *To Have and Have Not* as an example. It resulted in Hawks'
1944 film that introduced Lauren Bacall to the screen, and to the film's
star, Humphrey Bogart, eventually resulting in future screen pairings and
a happy marriage. *To Have and Have Not* was one of the 30 top grossing
films of its year.

Screenwriter Ranald MacDougall scored big with his first screenplay,
Objective Burma (1945), and followed that up with such hits as *Mil-
dred Pierce* (1945) and *Possessed* (1947) both featuring Joan Crawford.
MacDougall told Jack Warner he wanted to do a new screen version of
Hemingway's *To Have and Have Not*, but not as a remake of the 1944
film. MacDougall wanted to write a screenplay that was much closer

to the original source material, and star John Garfield in the lead. Garfield wanted to play the role, but requested that Michael Curtiz direct. Garfield recalled having worked with Curtiz while under contract for Warners some ten years earlier, and believed the director helped make him a star. Curtiz had directed *Mildred Pierce*, so he was familiar with MacDougall's work. Studio head Jack Warner approved.

John Garfield was also offered a new Warner Brothers contract which would allow him the creative freedom he coveted upon leaving the studio a few years earlier. Hits like *Body and Soul* and *Force of Evil* had made a difference, indicating that, unlike some actors, Garfield was a real success with his own production company (compare that to James Cagney, whose indie productions with brother Bill were such that Cagney returned to the studio and ended up making *White Heat*, one of his biggest hits). Garfield's new contract with Warners would have him make two pictures a year, over the next five years, and could possibly net him $3 million. He would be allowed the freedom to do independent deals with his own company.

Another consideration this time was John Garfield's health. Having suffered a heart attack that caused a three-week delay in a previous production had to be considered. According to the press:

> Representatives of John Garfield are irked by reports about the actor being in Arizona, asserting that he is still in New York and that he has been given clearance by his doctors. The actor, it is said, will be ready to embark on *The Breaking Point* at Warners in February. It might be noted that this picture is really the story of rum-smuggling in the Caribbean, which was told in the Ernest Hemingway novel, *To Have and Have Not*. The film of that title with Humphrey Bogart, that introduced Lauren Bacall, was freely adapted, bearing little resemblance, therefore, to the original. Meanwhile Bob Roberts has the gambling saga, *The Man With the Golden Arm*, in good shape for Garfield by the time the actor is ready to resume with his independent organization.[86]

Once everything was agreed to and settled, *The Breaking Point* began filming, and John Garfield turned in yet another of his finest performances.

John Garfield plays Harry Morgan, a fishing boat captain who is having business troubles which leave him wallowing in debt and having trouble providing for his wife (Phyllis Thaxter) and two daughters (Donna Jo Boyce, Sherry Jackson). A shifty lawyer named Duncan (Wallace Ford) talks Harry into smuggling some Chinese men from Mexico to California. But things go wrong and Harry gets in a fight with the lawyer's

86 John Garfield's Health Reported Okay. *The Los Angeles Times.* January 14, 1950

Victor Sen Yung, Wallace Ford, and John Garfield create a scheme in The Breaking Point.

accomplice, Mr. Sing (Victor Sen Yung) who is thrown overboard to his death. This allows Duncan to blackmail Harry into helping a group of crooks escape a racetrack robbery via his boat. While Harry is waiting on his boat for Duncan and the criminals to arrive, his partner Wesley (Juano Hernandez) comes by. Harry tries to get rid of him, but is unsuccessful, and when the crooks arrive, they shoot and kill Wesley. Harry is then forced at gunpoint to continue as planned, but en route he grabs a couple of guns he had hidden on the boat, and gets into a gunfight with the criminals, killing them, but also getting seriously injured himself. Harry's wife rushes to him at the hospital, where Harry must agree to allow surgeons to amputate his arm in order to save his life.

One of the pivotal points in *The Breaking Point* is Harry's attraction to Leona Charles (Patricia Neal), who is alluring and flirtatious. She and her much older beau Hannagan (Ralph Dumke) hire Harry's boat for fishing, but Hannagan skips out on paying, leaving Leona behind. Harry does not have the necessary docking fee, and that leads to the desperate Harry to break the law and accept Duncan's smuggling scheme. John Garfield keeps Harry grounded as he gradually gets in deeper as a result of varying degrees of desperation. He needs the immediate money for docking, he needs long term funds to help support his family, and he sees a way to do one unlawful thing and have enough money to perhaps

John Garfield is distracted by alluring Patricia Neal in The Breaking Point.

expand his business to a fleet of fishing boats. Harry is so desperate for his dreams, he convinces himself that bad decisions are necessary.

Harry is drawn to Leona as something of a distraction. His wife and children are his base, and he loves them, but he is unsettled by his inability to provide for them, and has to deal with his wife, who wants him to sell his boat and pursue regular employment elsewhere. Harry realizes his dream isn't coming true, but balks at releasing his dream. This hardened reality is such that he allows himself to be romantically distracted by the alluring Leona the same way he succumbs to the opportunity provided by Duncan.

Neal is wonderful in this movie, as is Phyllis Thaxter, as Harry's wife Lucy who was a nice foil to Neal's character. She appeared to know that Neal was a threat, but stood by her husband despite her concerns. The early scenes in this movie establish the relationship between Lucy and Harry well. Financially struggling, Garfield conveys with his body language (he's kind of slumped over and not really facing his wife head-on as he talks to her) how ashamed Harry is that he is having trouble providing for his family. This also makes it understandable why Harry decides to take the risks he does later on.

The complexity of the Harry Morgan character is one of the most creative challenges John Garfield would enjoy as a movie actor. In what would turn out to be his penultimate film, Garfield was able to call upon his penchant for bitter anger, romantic tenderness, smoldering sensuality, and heroic action. It resulted in a bravura performance that even Garfield himself considered perhaps his best work.

Garfield had a lot of input into his character, further indicating how involved and invested he was in crafting his projects. According to Stephanie Zacharek's Criterion essay on *The Breaking Point*, Garfield wrote to Curtiz making suggestions such as the inclusion of a detail from Hemingway's novel in which Harry brings home gifts for his wife and daughters from his travels, because it would make Harry more human.

Garfield persuaded the screenwriter to take two of the Hemingway characters from the story – shipmates Albert and Eddie – and merge them into the character of Wesley, a trustworthy friend and mate, played by Juano Hernandez. The character of Wesley, according to film noir historian Eddie Muller, "happened to be black." Muller continued:

> The filmmakers made Wesley a regular guy – loyal, wise, and patient – not a symbol of noble black suffering. And to make Harry and Wesley equals, MacDougall gave Wesley a son, who is seen several times shyly interacting with Harry's daughters. These were crucial, but simple embellishments, and they make Wesley's pointless murder all the more devastating.[87]

The short amount of time of those scenes make it clear that Wesley is more than just Harry's partner, he is his best friend. When Wesley is killed, we see how devastated Harry is in Garfield's eyes. The final shot of Wesley's son (played by actor Hernandez's real life son) coming on the dock looking for his father is one of the most heartbreaking final shots in any movie. There is so much hustle and bustle going on at the dock centered around Harry and the other white characters, that nobody appears to notice this little African American boy, and nobody stops to tell him what happened to his father. And his father was killed as a result of Harry's—a white man—decision-making. It's devastating.

Unfortunately, shortly before the film's release, John Garfield's troubles with the HUAC, and his being perceived as a Communist, became too much for Warner Brothers to deal with. According to Garfield's biographer: "There was no more talk of a new contract offer from Warners, and ominously and suddenly, there were no offers at all. The telephone stopped ringing. Scripts stopped coming his way."[88]

---

87   Muller, Eddie. Noir Alley broadcast on Turner Classic Movies. July 25, 2020.
88   Swindell, Larry. Body and Soul: The Story of John Garfield. NY: Morrow. 1975

Also, during the filming of *The Breaking Point*, Louella Parsons' column wrote that talks between Garfield, Roberts, and Nelson Algren had broken down:

> More trouble over *The Man With the Golden Arm* which John Garfield bought. The author, Nelson Algren, who was supposed to come to Hollywood to write the screenplay, has now backed out because he refuses to make the changes Bob Roberts, the producer, insists are necessary to overcome the censorable angles. Both Roberts and Garfield claim they have a legal commitment for the property and have already spent a great deal of money preparing it, and now Algren is not only refusing to come to Hollywood but he wants to get out of the whole deal.[89]

The Man With The Golden Arm was eventually made by Otto Preminger, who defied studio parameters and allowed Algren to write the script without the sanitizing changes insisted upon by Roberts. John Garfield had died by then, so the lead went to Frank Sinatra. It is one of the singer's finest acting performances in films.

Because of the studio's indifference, *The Breaking Point* was not given much publicity and, thus, performed poorly at the box office. But it remains one of the actor's finest performances, while Ernest Hemingway considered it the best screen adaptation of any of his stories.

Bob Roberts and John Garfield finally did find a project for their own production company, producing independently for release by United Artists.

---

89 Louella Parsons Column. Hearst Syndicate. March 15, 1950

HE RAN ALL THE WAY

Directed by John Berry
Screenplay by Dalton Trumbo and Hugo Butler (billed as Guy Endore)
from the novel by Sam Ross.
Produced by Bob Roberts and John Garfield
Cinematography by James Wong Howe
Edited by Harry Horner

Cast:
John Garfield, Shelley Winters, Wallace Ford, Selena Royle Gladys
George, Norman Lloyd, Robert Hyatt, Clancy Cooper, Vici Raaf, Keith
Hetherington, Robert Karnes, Lucile Sewall, Dale Van Sickel, Renny
McEvoy, Ralph Brooks, John Morgan, Arthur Berkeley, Chet Branden-
burg, John Breen, James Magill, Monty O'Grady, Jimmy Ames, Gordon
Armitage, Willie Bloom, Johnny Duncan, A Cameron Grant, Joe Hinds,
Shep Houghton, Mark Lowell, William H. O'Brien, Charles Perry.

Released July 13, 1951
Roberts Pictures, inc. for United Artists
Running time: 77 minutes
Black and White

While it is a tragedy that John Garfield died so young, his final film
is an appropriate culmination to the trajectory of his career. In his first
film, *Four Daughters*, he suddenly appeared as an attractive, tumultuous
presence that disrupted the lives of a grounded family structure. In *He
Ran All The Way*, he does roughly the same thing, only this time his rebellious character is also a criminal who holds a simple working class family
hostage.

John Garfield plays Nick Robey, a small-time crook who plots with
his friend Al Molin (Norman Lloyd) to rob a man at a train yard for the
company payroll. While committing the crime, they are discovered by
police who open fire. Al is shot but Nick shoots the cop and is able to get
away. He hides out at a public swimming pool and goes for a swim, the
money in his jacket pockets which is secured in a locker. While swimming he collides with a beginner named Peg Dobbs (Shelley Winters)
and he purposely connects with her, believing that if he is part of a couple

John Garfield and Shelley Winters have a tense relationship in He Ran All The Way.

and not alone, he'll be less conspicuous. He talks her into allowing him to take her home, and when there he meets her family. The parents and younger brother go out to a movie, but Peg and Nick stay behind. Nick is jittery and finally admits he is in trouble. When the family returns, he impulsively and desperately pulls out a gun and holds them hostage overnight until he believes himself in the clear and able to leave without notice. Nick doesn't want to hurt anyone, and the next morning as he plans to leave, he even gives the family some money for their trouble. However, his photo and identity are front page headlines because Al identified him before he died. Fred Dobbs, Peg's father (Wallace Ford), tries to hide the paper from Nick so he'll leave, but Nick stops to have a cup of coffee before going and sees Fred holding the newspaper behind his back. Nick then stays hidden at the house, telling the family to go about their business going to work, school, etc, but reminding them that a family member will be with him at all times and will be killed if anyone reveals his whereabouts. Peg and Nick's attraction to each other somehow continues through all this, but when she decides to buy a car so they can run away together, Nick becomes reactively paranoid, and demands to see the receipt. When Peg cannot produce it, he drags her down the stairs. When they get downstairs, Nick is shot by Fred Dobbs who is waiting

John Garfield in the foreground with Wallace Ford and Shelley Winters in the background as his character dies in the gutter in He Ran All The Way.

outside. Nick drops his gun, leaps for cover, Peg picks up the gun and shoots him dead.

All of the elements of John Garfield the actor are evident in *He Ran All The Way* – the double-crossed loyalist, the desperate paranoiac who caves in to impulse, the bitter streetwise criminal who never caught a break, even the underlying tenderness beneath the gruff exterior. And while the hostage plot was considered cliché even as early as 1951, the script and performances make *He Ran All The Way* a strong, gritty melodrama. Somehow, despite playing a truly unscrupulous character, Garfield makes Nick sympathetic. He assumes control of the family, but at the same time is trapped. And there is no animosity or uncaring aloofness. When the mother (Selena Royle) is injured while sewing, Nick carries her to the couch and comforts her. Even when the young boy of the family (Bobby Hyatt) angrily lashes out, Nick patiently allows the child to punch at him until he is fatigued.

The film creates some sympathy for Nick in its opening scenes with him in the apartment he shares with his mother (Gladys George), being verbally abused by her. It's apparent from the start that he has likely had a rough upbringing. Perhaps he sees the kind of nice family he could have had in Peg's family, which is why he tries to do things for them like buy dinner even as he is holding them hostage. There's a sad sort of loneliness to him and it appears he sees their life and wonders what he might have achieved had his own circumstances been different. And while Nick is a petty crook who just got in over his head, Garfield brings a volatile nature to his character that adds a lot of tension to the movie; you never know when he's going to explode or what he's going to do, even when it's apparent that he likely won't actually hurt the family

But despite an element of sympathy for Nick, our sympathies are especially centered upon the hapless family. Peg continues to feel guilty remorse for allowing Nick into the house – by not recognizing his volatility which was already revealed in the swimming pool when he grabs her arm to the point of hurting her while making a point. Fred is torn between cooperating to avoid danger, and wanting to overpower the situation as the man of the house. The wife is frightened and cooperative. The son is defiantly bratty with childlike confusion.

In one of the movie's most tense scenes, Nick orders dinner for the family and goes all out by ordering a complete turkey dinner. However, Mrs. Dobbs quietly makes stew unbeknownst to Nick, and serves that to the family. Nick redirects her, stating that he bought the turkey dinner for the entire family. But for once he is challenged. Fred Dobbs tells him, "That's your food. This is ours." Both confused and offended by this challenge, believing he made a nice gesture, Nick tries to force the family, at gunpoint, to join him. He even fires a shot. The Dobbs family continues to stand up to him.

The actors are significantly good and powerful in their roles. Shelley Winters turns in a magnificent performance, and vividly recalls her experience making the film in her book *Shelley II: The Middle of My Century*:

> The time frame of *He Ran All the Way* covered twelve hours. It starts in the early afternoon in a swimming pool. James Wong Howe's camera was at the side of the pool above the water. The director had arranged for a stuntman double to do Garfield's swimming. Garfield had had a severe heart attack at the Beverly Hills Tennis Club a few months earlier. I knew that underwater swimming was especially taxing to the heart. I rehearsed with the double, but when we came to the actual shooting of the scene, Garfield refused to let the double do it. We had to do the scene about ten times to get the lighting in the water right. It was scary and unnecessary...Back then, I could not understand why John insisted on doing this dangerous shot himself. In retrospect, it seems almost as if he unconsciously wanted another heart attack.

I didn't understand the political trouble he was in. I just knew that Warner Brothers, by breaking his contract and casting him adrift, were destroying one of their most valuable properties and breaking his heart. He was generous to me in every way a big star can be to a newcomer. He gave me the best camera angles in two-shots, made sure the camera favored me and the audience saw both of my eyes. He spent hours on my close-ups, and if he didn't like the rushes and felt I could look prettier, he insisted that the director relight the scene and reshoot it. *He Ran All The Way* was one of the most remarkable and important films I was ever to do.[90]

Shelley Winters lost 15 pounds in a week in order to be cast in the role. It helped to further advance her growing career. She's very convincing as this sort of naïve young woman; it's a very different kind of role from a lot of the brassy characters she'd play later in her career.

Wallace Ford had brilliantly played the unscrupulous Duncan in *The Breaking Point*, and reveals his remarkable versatility with his equally outstanding performance in a much different role in *He Ran All The Way*. Fred Dobbs struggles with the perception of his manhood. On one hand, Dobbs just wants to get through this and get it over with. On the other hand, he feels emaciated by the perception of himself as weak. When Dobbs refuses to partake in the turkey dinner, he has reached the point where he must take a stand.

Anti-Communist sentiment was at a real high in America with the outset of the Korean Conflict, which only strengthened the HUAC. John Garfield continued to garner publicity for having been a member of the Committee for the First Amendment, which opposed governmental investigation of Communist activity in Hollywood, and the fact that his wife had been a member of the Communist party. As a result, he had to underwrite this film with his own funds. Director John Berry and screenwriters Dalton Trumbo and Hugo Butler had their names removed from the credits due to being blacklisted, which is why the screenplay is credited to Guy Endore, and the director is sometimes credited as Emmett Emerson, the film's assistant director.

He Ran All The Way was not a box office success, which disappointed John Garfield, who had supported it with his own money. Shortly after its completion, Garfield was called to testify before the HUAC, which he did, but refused to name names. Reportedly, they wanted him to name his wife. They asked how actress Anne Revere voted, and Garfield replied,

---

90 Winters, Shelley. *Shelley II: The Middle of My Century*. NY: Simon and Schuster, 1989

"I know how I voted." The questioning covered Garfield's entire career, from the Warner Brothers years, to his independent production, and then to his involvement with everything from the Screen Actors Guild to the various organizations that were considered sympathetic to Communism, although the actor himself was never a member of the Communist party. John Garfield denounced Communism and proclaimed himself a liberal, stating, "I don't think Communists like Liberals very much, and I was very outspoken in my Liberalism."[91]

Garfield's daughter Julie later stated: "My father's stand was basically: 'Ask me anything you want about myself. I'll tell you. But don't ask me about my wife and don't ask me about my friends.'" As a result, she says, "he was hounded by the FBI."[92] John Garfield stated to the HUAC:

> When I was originally requested to appear before the committee, I said that I would answer all questions, fully and without any reservations, and that is what I have done. I have nothing to be ashamed of and nothing to hide. My life is an open book. I was glad to appear before you and talk with you. I am no Red. I am no pink. I am no fellow traveler. I am a Democrat by politics, a liberal by inclination, and a loyal citizen of this country by every act of my life.[93]

The press called John Garfield's testimony naïve, and the *Daily Worker* called him a traitor. George Sokolsy wrote in his syndicated column:

> When a witness appears before a congressional committee, he adopt the attitude that was called because he has something to contribute or that he was called because the committee wants to get something on him. Certainly, those who are called in the Communist cases often feel embarrassed by the subpoena, for there is always the fear that the public might assume that being called for evidence is being accused of subversion. John Garfield, the motion picture actor, went to the House committee on unAmerican activities accompanied by his lawyer, Louis Nizer, and by public relations counsel and his testimony was glibly and cleverly told, but there was in it something that I do not understand. Here it is: John Garfield said that he went out to Hollywood in 1938. So, he was asked by Rep. Velde: "When did you first come to this realization that there was a Communist party in Hollywood?"

---

91 Swindell, Larry. Body and Soul: The Story of John Garfield. NY: Morrow. 1975
92 Day, Crosby. Garfield: An Actor Who Stood His Ground. Orlando Sentinel. February 7, 2003
93 From original court transcripts

Mr. Garfield: "As I said before, when I quit the Wallace thing. I felt he was being captured by a group of Communists."

Mr. Velde: You didn't know before that time that there was a Communist party organization in Hollywood?

Mr. Garfield: I did not

Mr Velde: Approximately what date did you decide there was a Communist movement in Hollywood?

Mr. Garfield: Late 1947 or 1948.

How could any man be in Hollywood, be situated there, live there, read the newspapers and not know that there was a Communist movement in Hollywood between 1938 and 1948? I should like to know how the whole history of those 10 years could be missed by John Garfield or by anyone else who can read. So, Rep. Jackson got into it and this colloquy occurred:

Mr Jackson: And you contend that during the seven and one-half years or more that you were in Hollywood and in close contact with a situation in which a number of Communist cells were operating on a week-to-week basis, with electricians, actors, and every class represented, that during the entire period of time you were in Hollywood you did not know of your own personal knowledge a member of the Communist party?

Mr. Garfield: That is absolutely correct, because I was not a party member or associated in any shape, way or form.

Mr. Jackson: It might interest you to know attempts were made to recruit me into the Communist party, and I was making $32.50 a week.

Mr. Garfield: They certainly stayed away from me, sir.

I do not say that Mr. Garfield is or is not a Communist. I do not know and I am not called to sit in judgment. Nor do I question the veracity of his statements. Nor can he assuage my doubts that any man who lives in cities like New York or Hollywood, who moves in intellectual circles, who gives evidence of being literate and intelligent, could possibly live between the years 1938 and 1948 and not know anything at all about a Communist movement in Hollywood. Maybe it is possible, but as Mr. Jackson said, I am not convinced.

Rep. Jackson said: "I do say that for one who is as intelligent and as well qualified as this witness has proven himself to be, it shows a naive or unintelligent approach to this problem for him to contend that he could have lived with this activity 10, 11 or 15 years and not know more about it than he acknowledges."

It just does not ring the bell.[94]

One career bright spot during this period was the opportunity to finally star in the lead role of Joe Bonaparte in a stage revival of Clifford Odets' *Golden Boy*. Playing the role that had originally been written for him, but had been denied him on stage and on film, John Garfield eagerly accepted the job. It was not only a chance to work, it was a chance to finally play one of his most coveted role. And just as *He Ran All The Way* was to be John Garfield's final film, *Golden Boy* would be his final stage performance.

---

94 John Garfield's Testimony Before Committee Didn't Ring Bell. King Features Syndicate. May 9, 1951

THE FINAL YEAR

The revival of *Golden Boy* opened for a limited engagement of four weeks on March 12, 1952. However, it was so popular, its engagement continued for an extended three weeks. However, the HUAC situation and the blacklisting continued to stress John Garfield, and this was compounded by the deaths of friends Mady Christians, J. Edward Bromberg, and Canada Lee, all after they were blacklisted by the HUAC. Plans for John Garfield to appear in *Golden Boy* on television opposite Kim Stanley for CBS were cancelled. According to his daughter Julie Garfield, "They did one scene. And then CBS canceled it."[95]

John Garfield discovered that the HUAC was investigating his testimony for possible perjury charges. He was further haunted by the testimonies of Elia Kazan, who named names in April of 1952, and his friend Clifford Odets doing the same the next month. Attempting to denounce Communism once and for all, John Garfield arranged to pen a feature article for *Look* magazine, to be entitled "I was a Sucker for a Left Hook," which referred to his noted boxing films and plays. It was a desperate attempt to salvage his reputation. At about the same time, May of 1952, John Garfield moved out of his family home, some claiming the separation from his wife was due to the 16 page article he penned for *Look*.

Later that month, on May 20th, Garfield was having dinner with his friend Iris Whitney when he stated he felt uneasy and sickly. Garfield had played a few strenuous rounds of tennis against his doctor's orders, and had not slept the night before. Whitney brought him to her apartment where he was able to lie down. She wanted to call a doctor, but Garfield refused. The next morning, Iris Whitney found John Garfield dead. His death was attributed to long term heart problems, but many have claimed the stress of the blacklisting contributed to his fatal heart attack. Garfield never knew that, only a day before his death, the HUAC cleared him. His friend Clifford Odets cooperated with the HUAC but also reaffirmed that John Garfield was never a member of the Communist party.

---

95 Weinraub, Bernard. Recalling John Garfield, Rugged Star KO'd by Fate. *The New York Times*. January 30, 2003

John Garfield died in May of 1952 at the age of 39.

John Garfield's daughter Julie later stated: "My father didn't die angry. He was more devastated, sad, overwhelmed and terribly hurt. If he had been more angry, I think that could have left him alive and fighting."[96]

John Garfield's funeral was the biggest in New York since Rudolph Valentino's some 25 years earlier. Over ten thousand people crowded the

---

96 Day, Crosby. Garfield: An Actor Who Stood His Ground. Orlando Sentinel. February 7, 2003

streets. He was buried at Westchester Hills Cemetery in Hastings-on-Hudson, Westchester County, New York.

Prior to his passing there was interest in casting John Garfield in the play *The Fragile Fox*, which, in 1956, became the film *Attack!* directed by Robert Aldrich, who had been assistant director on *Body and Soul*. Another stage success, *The Big Knife*, was also filmed by Aldrich, the year earlier. Meanwhile, John Garfield's legacy continued to resonate through the work of actors like Montgomery Clift, Marlon Brando, and James Dean, who became especially popular as the 1950s continued.

John Garfield entered movies during the golden age of 1930s Hollywood and through the war years, maintained stardom at a major studio. During the post-war era he investigated independent production and explored cinema's auteurist approach to his work. His early death has unfortunately caused him to be less known in the 21st century than he should be, but his towering influence as an actor continues to be felt with every brooding rebel on the screen.

BIBLIOGRAPHY

Books

Agee, James. *Agree on Film*. NY: Grosset and Dunlap, 1969

Auerbach, Jonathan *Dark Borders: Film Noir and American Citizenship*. Duke University Press. 2011

Bacall, Lauren. *By Myself*. NY: Knopf, 1979

Beaver, Jim. *John Garfield: His Life and Films*. Cranbury, NJ: A.S. Barnes & Co. 1978

Behlmer, Rudy. *Inside Warner Brothers* NY: Viking, 1985

Davidson, Bill. *Spencer Tracy: Tragic Idol*. NY: Dutton. 1988

Dolan, Edward F. Jr. *Hollywood Goes to War*. London: Bison Books, 1985.

Eliot, Marc. *Cary Grant: A Biography*. New York: Aurum Press, 2005.

Gosse, Van. Where the Boys are: Cuba, Cold War America and the Making of a New Left. London: Verso, 1993

Henreid, Paul and Julius Fast. *Ladies Man: An Autobiography*. NY: St Martin's Press, 1984

Hirschorn, Clive. *The Warner Brothers Story*. NY: Crown. 1987

Orriss, Bruce. *When Hollywood Ruled the Skies: The Aviation Film Classics of World War II*. Hawthorne, California: Aero Associates Inc., 1984

McGrath, Patrick J. *John Garfield: The Illustrated Career in Films And on Stage*. Jefferson, NC: McFarland & Co. 2006

Morris, George. *John Garfield*. New York, Jove Publications, 1977

Nott, Robert. *He Ran All The Way: The Life of John Garfield*. NY: Limelight. 2003

Rode, Alan K. *Michael Curtiz: A Life in Film*. University Press of Kentucky, 2017

Sennett, Ted. *Warner Brothers Presents* NY: Arlington House. 1971

Swindell, Larry. *Body and Soul: The Story of John Garfield*. NY: Morrow. 1975

Winters, Shelley. *Shelley II: The Middle of My Century*. NY: Simon and Schuster, 1989

Articles and Reviews

122 Degrees. Silver Screen. January, 1939

Blackwell's Island review. Film Daily. March 2, 1939

Blackwell's Island review. The New York Times. March 2, 1939

Body and Soul review. The New York Times. November 10, 1947

Cameron, Kate. Tortilla Flat review. New York Daily News. May 22, 1942

Crowther, Bosley. Saturday's Children review. The New York Times. May 4, 1940

Crowther, Bosley Tortilla Flat review. The New York Times, May 22, 1942

Daughters Courageous Due to Open. Oakland Tribune. July 26, 1939

Cow Milking Actors Rare. Oakland Tribune. June 6, 1939

Crow, James Francis. Reviews and Previews. Los Angeles Evening Citizen News. June 6, 1941

Crowther, Bosley. Between Two Worlds review. The New York Times. May 6, 1944

Dangerously They Live review. Film Daily. December 24, 1941

Dangerously They Live review. Motion Picture Daily. December 23, 1941

Daves Will Direct Story of Al Schmid. Los Angeles Times. October 5, 1944

Day, Crosby. Garfield: An Actor Who Stood His Ground. Orlando Sentinel. February 7, 2003

Double Premier for Sea Wolf. San Francisco Examiner. March 15, 1941.

East of the River review. The Movies and the People Who Make Them. November 9, 1940

Erskine Johnson column. Los Angeles Daily News. January 8, 1947

Fallen Sparrow Review. Film Daily. August 20, 1943

Film Noir. Encyclopedia Brittanica (as quoted in….)

Four Daughters review. The New York Times. August 19, 1938

Garfield Ends Three-Months Balk. Pomona Progress Bulletin. January 1, 1940

Garfield Fears Fame Will Make Him Forget Dreams. San Francisco Examiner. May 21, 1939

Garfield Recalled by Successors at Patri School. Los Angeles Times. February 20, 1940

Gentleman's Agreement review. Variety. November 11, 1947

Harry Mines column. Los Angeles Daily News February 9, 1943

Hollywood with Fredric Othman. Chico Record. October 19, 1941

Hedda Hopper column. Los Angeles Times. June 7, 1944

John Garfield's Testimony Before Committee Didn't Ring Bell. King Features Syndicate. May 9, 1951

Juarez – The Life History of a Movie. Photoplay. June, 1939

Louella Parsons column. Hearst Syndicate. June 6, 1938, June 10, 1942, June 21, 1949, March 15, 1950

Many Roles Lined Up For Garfield. Los Angeles Times. July 8, 1938.

Nobody Lives Forever review. San Francisco Examiner October 9, 1946

Parsons, Louella. Olivia Defies Studio Order, Is Suspended. International News Service (syndicated). December 21, 1939

Paul Harrison in Hollywood. NEA syndicate. January 9, 1939, June 23, 1939

Pride of the Marines review. New York Times. August 25, 1945

Pride of the Marines review. Variety August 31, 1945

Saturday's Children. Showmen's Trade Review May 4, 1940

Saturday's Children review. Film Daily. April 17, 1940

Schallert, Edwin. Postman Always Rings Twice review. Los Angeles Times. May 8, 1946

Scheuer, Phillip K. Tucker's People. Los Angeles Times. June 13, 1948

Scott, John. Navy Sees Preview in Submarine. Los Angeles Times. December 23, 1943

Sea Wolf review. Film Daily. March 24, 1941

Sea Wolf review. Motion Picture Daily. March 24, 1941

Soans, Wood. Six-Year Contract With Warper's Will Allow Four Appearances in New York. Oakland Tribune. July 24, 1940

Television Documentaries Planned. The Los Angeles Times. June 23, 1948

Thomson, David. What is the Most Dangerous Film in History? The New Republic. July 29, 2012

Topics For Gossip. Silver Screen. September, 1939

Under My Skin review. The New York Times. March 18, 1950

Walker, Paul. Reviews and Previews. Harrisburg Telegraph. September 18, 1939.

Walter Winchell On Broadway. New York Daily Mirror. December 2, 1940

Ward Soans Column. Oakland Tribune. January 16, 1941

Warners Aid Scraps. Motion Picture Daily. December 15, 1943

Warners Will Star Robinson in Remake of The Sea Wolf. The San Francisco Examiner. May 30, 1940

We Were Strangers review. *Modern Screen*. May, 1949

Weinraub, Bernard. Recalling John Garfield, Rugged Star KO'd by Fate. The New York Times. January 30, 2003

What The Picture Did For Me. Motion Picture Herald. Various Issues.

Internet sources

Hoberman, J. The Jewish Brando. Tablet. March 3, 2013

Passafiume, Andrea. Fallen Sparrow Review. TCM.com

Morgan, Kim. Happy 100th Birthday John Garfield. Sunset Gun website. March 4, 2013

The Sea Wolf: Longer and Better. Leonard Maltin's Movie Crazy. October 25, 2017

Self Styled Siren: The Year in Old Movies by Farran Nehme. December 29, 2018

Smith, Imogen Sara. Plumbing the Depths of Capitalism in Force of Evil. *Bright Lights Film Journal.* July 31, 2008

Television

Muller, Eddie. Noir Alley broadcast of The Breaking Point on Turner Classic Movies. July 25, 2020.

INDEX